JUMPING THROUGH LIFE'S HURDLES WITH A SMILE

You Can Only Play The Hand You're Dealt

ROBERT COHEN

JUMPING THROUGH LIFE'S HURDLES WITH A SMILE
YOU CAN ONLY PLAY THE HAND YOU'RE DEALT

iUniverse books may be ordered through booksellers or by contacting:

iUniverse
1663 Liberty Drive
Bloomington, IN 47403
www.iuniverse.com
1-800-Authors (1-800-288-4677)

Scripture quotations from the Holy Bible, King James Version (Authorized Version). First published in 1611. Quoted from the KJV Classic Reference Bible.

Scripture quotations marked NLT are taken from the Holy Bible, New Living Translation, copyright © 1996, 2004, 2007. Used by permission of Tyndale House Publishers, Inc. Carol Stream, Illinois 60188. All rights reserved. Website

Scripture quotations marked NIV are taken from the Holy Bible, New International Version®. NIV®. Copyright © 1973, 1978, 1984 by International Bible Society. Used by permission of Zondervan. All rights reserved. [Biblica]

Scripture quotations marked NKJV are taken from the New King James Version. Copyright © 1982 by Thomas Nelson, Inc. Used by permission. All rights reserved.

ISBN: 978-1-5320-8648-9 (sc)
ISBN: 978-1-5320-8649-6 (e)

Print information available on the last page.

iUniverse rev. date: 02/25/2020

Contents

Introduction

Love Inspiration and Aspiration

Love, inspiration, and aspiration. The love aspect is one that should be taken very earnestly in order to inspire the aspirations of a person to come forward. When people have love, inspiration, and aspirations, it encourages people to get the drive to do something. Your love for your life will not waver at anyone who has a will to get up and live their life with a purpose or will attempt to get up and go out to find a job and do something that gives them purpose. Love will give you the drive to persevere into your inspiration and cause you to have an aspiration, because your life is too valuable to give up on. In today's society there are not enough people trying to make an attempt to go after your aspirations. Dreams can become dormant and God can take the gifts he's given to you and give them to some someone who will use them.

#Love Inspiration &Aspiration Brings About Determination

Cherish

By: Robert Cohen

To cherish something means that you greatly appreciate the value. When you cherish something you should not only greatly appreciate it but you should also keep it close to your heart and treat it with the utmost respect. It is special and in some cases it could be the only thing that keeps you going from day to day.

Challenges

By: Robert E. Cohen
6/20/16

In life everyone will encounter challenges at some point. When challenges arise, it's not the challenge that we face but it's how we handle the challenge that is important. It is important to handle the challenge with careful consideration of everything and everyone involved in the challenge to ensure that it is handled the best way possible for all people. Challenges never inform you of when they're coming, they just come and you have to handle it the best way you know how, with the best judgement you can. Do not get discouraged because the challenge will not last but a little while and at the end you will smile.

Thoughts
2/27/2017

Thoughts are how we process what goes on in our mind. Some thoughts are good thoughts; some thoughts are bad thoughts. Some are happy thoughts; some thoughts are sad thoughts. Thoughts sometimes can confuse you when you're going through your battles but thoughts about your life should always be taken very seriously and step by step. Never overthink your thoughts.

Always look toward what you to come to fruition out of the thoughts before you take action.

Thoughts should be taken very literally and very seriously; thoughts of love thoughts of kindness. The way you feel about yourself will determine how you interact with others. So always be careful about how you treat people and what your thoughts are toward everything you go through.

The Vulnerability Factor

1/12/2018
A Poem by <u>Robert Cohen</u>

As human beings we sometimes can be so loving and kind toward others. Yet, we don't always realize that people don't always have the best interest at heart. We have to be careful about how close we get to the people because people sometimes take advantage of things when they don't think you know better. God always have an angel in place looking out for you. God will always have a way out before you get too far into it. We don't always realize God is trying to show us a way out but in 2018 we must try our best not to be used, abused, and mistreated by those people. God will handle them in his own time. #BetterNewYear

The Search for Love

By: Robert E. Cohen
Aug.04, 2017

The search for love can be interesting but very difficult at the same time. There are several variables that you have to consider when beginning the search for love.

First of all, it's good to have a relationship with God for yourself before you pray. Ask God for the relationship that you desire.

You must pray and seek God asking Him for the wisdom, to guide you to the person that He has for you. Many times this is where we go wrong because we hardly ever seek God first for a relationship.

And if we don't ask Him there's no way for him to lead us and guide us in the right direction to find the person that we hope to be our soulmate.

You have to know what you are looking for in a person and once you find that person you have to sit down with them and discuss what exactly will be expected out of each other in the relationship.

Love is a game of chess. You have to carefully work your way through the relationship without damaging and carefully seek what you want from the relationship. Make sure the both of you are in the same mindset for seeking the relationship because if that's out of whack everything else will be out of whack.

The Destruction of Cancer

1/12/2018

A Poem by <u>Robert Cohen</u>

Cancer is killing people at a rapid rate. We must do what we can to prevent people from dying. We must help those suffering with this disease and those who have already passed by researching to find a cure. #Curemustcomesoon

The Repressed Feelings of Sadness During Grief

1/12/2018

A Poem by <u>Robert Cohen</u>

Confused feelings of a difficult season in my life
A season where my world is seemingly destroyed
A season where I lost two very closed loved ones
A season where I really need God's help and guidance to get me through
A trying storm in my life
A season where the last half of the year has been very dark for me
But God has not let me let go of him, he will not allow me to lose my mind because I am strong and my break through is right around the corner
In 2018 I shall reach the turning point and my break through and all the success God wants me to have will come to light and God will get all of the glory out of my success
Now and forever in Jesus name Amen

Procrastination

November 7, 2017
By: Robert E. Cohen

Procrastination is something that slows you down from your destiny. When you procrastinate things, things take forever to get done. Procrastination is a detrimental thing to certain situations. When you procrastinate, you are trying to get something done at the last second. It is not always necessary. If you know about it and get it done early, that will be one less thing on your plate. So whatever you do, try your best not to procrastinate because it may cause an interference of someone getting to their destiny.

One Day

1/17/18
By: Robert E. Cohen

One day when I see my dreams alive

God has blessed me so much I can't stop thanking

Him for everything he has done.

Don't give up on your hopes and your dreams

The power and the patience he has given me

Whatever you are trying to accomplish

Do it.

No Limits

Robert Cohen
July 24, 2017

Today, we as people tend to place limits on the things that we can do.

We should always make the effort to make things happen because when you place limits on yourself you are then limiting your opportunities that you may receive in life.

As an individual with a physical disability, I place no limits on my life or my abilities of what I can and cannot do.

If you set your mind to do something, it can be done.

It may just take a little more effort, but if you're willing to work it will be done.

People should never say what they can and can't do because life is filled with challenges: some being harder than others.

Yet with the help of god and your own personal effort, even if it is not perfect you can at least say that you tried.

With that attempt to accomplish, you shall feel confidence and God always honors a try.

There should be no limit placed on your life, because I put no limits on mine and I hope for the world to be inspired by me.

We should always remember that, you can encourage others just by trying and putting your mind into your situation to accomplish your goals.

Robert Cohen

Next Level

Wed March 14, 2018
Robert E. Cohen

The next level in my life is a very trying one, because right now I'm going through a season in my life when I'm dealing with loss, pain and trying to find love.

But one thing we must understand when finding love is that it's not an easy task. You have to find that special women; not just somebody that you can sleep with and have just a sexual relationship.

You need a friend that's going to be marriage material. Men, we got to stop looking for these sorry behind women that don't mean us any good. We got to find that one woman that we can get married to. I'm getting a bit too old to be bull-jiving; I need to settle down.

First of all, we need to get our relationship with God right, straighten ourselves out then maybe God will send the woman to us.

See our problem is we spend so much time looking that we can't see what's falling from the tree. Sometimes the tree you need is looking right at you. Sometimes we think the grass is greener on the other side and not looking at the right things. We got to look at the mind as well as physical. In next level 2018, I will be finding my wife.

In Jesus name, I'm going to find my wife!

My Heart Hurts

1/31/18
By: Robert E. Cohen

Y'all got to realize, y'all going to be taking care of

Not from security guards or police y'all going to be taking

Care of from the man upstairs.

Don't let nobody say you can't do nothing cause

If I can do it, you can too.

I lost two very important people in 2013 God

Will always protect his people. Don't look at what you see

It's more things to see in life.

Whatever you want to do don't let nobody stop you

From doing what you have to do.

My Dark Place

2/12/18
By: Robert E. Cohen

There is a dark place in me right now
That no one can see but God
I need his guidance to help me see where I am
Help me to better love people and help me not to lose focus and to not
have an attitude by things people say and the things people do
For I know that you will be there for me and protect me.
I know that there are earthly guardian angels looking out for me
Like Kiara and Temicia
I really thank you for blessing my life with them and other angels you
put in my life. I pray that you continue to guide me, bless me, and keep
me in your perfect peace while I go through difficult times.
Always in Jesus name amen.

Love in a Dark Place

2/16/18

Love is not always in the brightest place where you can see it

Sometimes love is hidden; hidden in the person looking for it b/c they're not certain of what they're looking for

A lot of times, we don't always know where to look for love

So we have to find ways to make love come to us so we're not constantly looking for it

One thing I know is in order to find love, you've got to have agape love that God gives all of us

Unconditional love that God bestows upon us everyday

Every day He breathes life into your lungs, you have love

And that's the love you need to be looking for in any type of relationship.

Life's Journey

By: Robert Cohen
March 4, 2018

Life's journey can sometimes be a very trying one, one where things can sometimes go haywire in a blink of an eye. I've had a trying middle to end of 2017. I've had two people really close to me pass away which was my mother and aunt and I've had trouble dealing with it. But God is still good no matter what. No matter what, He will bring me through it. And everything that he has done for me and will continue to do so for me it will be better in 2018. My books are starting to flourish and I love the direction my career is starting to take. All I can do is thank God for everything. God is really allowing my life to move forward in spite of the trials and tribulations I've had to face in this spring and summer of 2017 and it can only get better because God will continue to bless me so I can be a better blessing to others.

Confidence

Robert Cohen
March 21, 2017

Confidence is something everyone should have a measure of.

Confidence is something people should always be definite about.

Confidence should always be taken with stride but not pride.

Confidence should always be something that makes you put your best forward in everything and love yourself, because unless you love yourself you can't find a way to love anyone else.

The Breakdown

1/12/18
By: Robert E. Cohen

Within me are feelings of lost memories and people's love. I have uncontrollable tears and missing pieces of my heart that will never be found. God loves is the only things that can protect me through this situation.

Dear God, I need your guidance and strength in this trying time. I know your word say you will never leave me nor forsake me, so I'm asking you to help, guide, and protect me in this hard time. Amen in Jesus name I pray.

Greatness

by Robert Cohen
7/1/18

In life, there are two things you must do in order to succeed. Grow and learn how to be great. Not just physical growth, but growth of maturity too. Greatness is not measured by what you do, but by the potential kinetic energy that you put out in all of your endeavors. So attempt to be great in all you do and greatness will overcome you and all your endeavors. Then you would have no choice but to be great.

Success

by Robert Cohen
7/15/2018

The pursuit of success can sometimes be a very difficult and trying pursuit for people because everyone knows they want to be successful, but the issue is trying to figure out how to become successful because a lot of times people are unsure on how to make the dream of success come to fruition. What you cannot do is give up and allow the devil to overtake your mind and allow you to think that the things you are doing in an attempt to be successful is in vain, and that is simply not the case. Continue pursuing your endeavors and keep seeking God for wisdom for your next step because as long as you have breath in your body, there is always another opportunity in an attempt to be successful. #nevergiveup #keepstriving #anythingworthhavingisworthworkingtowards

Outcast

By: Robert Cohen
08/08/18

"I wrote this poem to inspire people that are feeling lonely."

Have you ever felt like you're an outcast in the world? Have you ever felt like people just didn't care? Have you ever felt like life is just passing you by and that you are all alone? Lately, I've been feeling mental sadness. My life is in shambles. About a month ago, my mother passed and I'm continuing to struggle even after I've been to brief counseling. It seems like nobody understands. I would feel better if someone in the physical would attempt to hear me out and assist me through my issues. It's difficult to find people whom I could trust or even open up to.

My Damaged Heart

By: Robert Cohen

"Something has a way of taking you through different stages to get you where God wants you to be."

Currently my heart is in intensive care, because at times I feel like I need to talk and there is no one there to listen, and that really hurts me. Because when people need me I am always there for them, but when the shoes is in the other foot they are nowhere to be found. I feel like God is moving me to my next level in him. When people need me I'm always found, but when I need them they are nowhere to be found. My damaged heart is really in need of intensive care, and me trying to keep my mind together is really hard. Because I really I don't want to give up, but with the down trodden second half of 2017 that I had with losing my Aunt and my mother 5 weeks apart is really hard. It is really hard and the fact that no one is there to listen to me that makes it that much worse. I just really wish that sometimes people would empathize with people who are different situations. And bare one another burdens as the Bible tells us too.

Determination

Life gives us opportunities to take advantage of certain situations

It's up to the individual to take advantage of the
situation God places in front of them

If you choose not to take advantage of that situation, then don't
waste your time complaining to God about missed opportunities

Time is one thing in life we can't get back

You must have a determined mind to take
advantage of the opportunities given to us

Finish Line

Life is a race that you

have to take slow and

with endurance. If you rush

through life, you often miss

opportunities and blessings

that God has in store for

you. In order to be prosperous,

you must pray and listen

to God and you will have

prosperity and success

in all you do.

Robert Cohen

Self-Love

Self-love is a must to live in this world and this earth daily because you would walk around like sour grapes with a negative attitude around everyone you encounter

God's Elevation

Life has a funny way of

showing us when God is

trying to elevate us to another level.

We don't always understand

why God takes things and

people out of our lives. When God

elevates people to new levels,

everyone can't go with you so

He has to remove those people

of your life. But when He does this,

you have to let those people go

because that blocks your blessings

if you remain in that season for

longer than you're supposed to

be there. So, let God control your

life and allow Him to

take you to the next level.

Robert Cohen

Smile through My Struggles

Sometimes you have to smile through your struggles to get through your day. Life is not always easy and you must take the time to smile b/c even through your struggles, your smile may bless somebody else. So, never deprive someone else of their blessing just b/c you're having a bad day. My struggles lately have been due to the death of my mom and my aunt taking place five weeks apart in 2017. And it seems like I've lost my ability to smile; my ability to want to do anything. It just seems like I'm going through the motions and I really want that part of my life back intact.

Dear Lord, I pray that you would restore every bad feeling I'm having and help me to get back to being the mighty man of God that you called me to be. So that when I get ready to do these shows, people will realize the inspiration that I am to everyone.

Amen.

Shine Your Light

In your life there are times when you must shine your light. And help other people to with their difficulties by your light. Because you never know how much just smiling at someone or asking them how they're doing will affect their day and you never know how much of a blessing you can be just by a few words. So always remember the things you do are always for you to shine your light for others and yourself. No matter what you do to try to keep a positive outlook on life. Negativity gains no one anything. Stay positive and stay encouraged in all you do.

Testimonials of Robert Cohen

"Our Brother, author of 5 books (with a new one coming out in December) and poet, Robert Cohen (SSU 🐾 Alum) came by to talk to the class and inspire them... but this part is going to get him killed by his twin sister!!! I told him!!! Lol" –Africanastudiesatssu

"He asked me to pray with him today within the first 2 minutes I had ever had a conversation with him. We talked for 30 straight minutes after that we were best friends. God knows how to always place the right people in your path. Robert has a beautiful soul, and is beautiful person inside and out....and he's an author with 4 books. Truly a blessing 🖤 " -Kayla Bailey

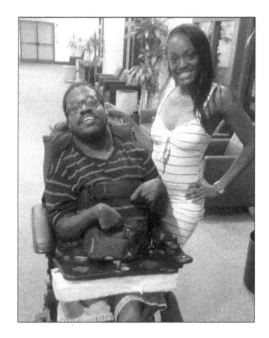

"I have no choice but to share with Facebook how much I admire Robert E. Cohen. Oftentimes, people go into depression or shut-down mode when dealing with hardships. I'm ashamed to say that I really don't know & I'm not sure, but I believe Robbie has cerebral palsy. However, he takes his diagnosis with stride and won't stop doing what he loves to do: motivating people. Many of you have probably walked past him in the mall w/o a second thought. I can't even recall how we became close, but those who know me, know we (my kid & I) talk to everyone. Despite being bound to a wheelchair, Robbie doesn't let his disability hinder his dreams, goals, and passion for reaching out to people. This young man has authored several books, preached sermons, done spoken word poetry, & those are just a few of his accomplishments. I say all of this to say, that we abled body people take so much for granted, & Robbie being the person he is prayed with/for me tonight & it was RIGHT ON TIME!!! I'm not going through anything & life is great at the moment, but the many times we've prayed together, I can truly say that tonight God sent him my way ... & for that my friend, I am forever grateful. Thanks Robbie 💜" -Tamika R. Blanchard.

"This is why I love Robert E. Cohen. I met Robert when I worked at Chick-fil-A in college. He used to always come buy a small lemonade and due to his disabilities he always required one of us to give him help alongside great customer service. Whenever I saw Robert coming, I had him! And no matter what he kept a smile on our faces. He became a close friend. Robert has overcome so many obstacles and accomplishments since then. First, his first book was published which I am very proud of. Please check it out. Secondly his mother passed away last year. For the past couple years, he has always kept in touch. Robert would call me in the middle of the night just to ask me to pray with him. His prayer would always be about god covering me and giving me the protection I needed to continue being great. Right now I'm on the road and by my surprise Robert calls and we prayed. The only thing he asks is for me to praise god in the middle of it. I just want to thank god for sending angels like Robert in my life. He serves the world well. Love you Robert♥"- Denise Lovely Perrbear

"I met Robert one day in the student union at our university (go orange and blue) and we immediately became friends. Robert is amazing and he is an inspiration to so many people, including myself. Once, at a dark time in my life, Robert called me and asked if I'd be willing to pray with him, he said he was compelled by God to do so. It's clear all his work has been ordained by God. Who do you know who fights as hard as him? He puts in work and seizes opportunities that most of us take advantage of. The Bible says you'll know a man by the fruits of his labor, and I'd say Robert's fruit shows how hard he works in the face of adversity. I thank God for him and I thank him for being obedient and reaching out to many with prayer and love. We all just need some love. I'm thankful his obedience has helped lead to my deliverance in Christ. Keep leading Robert. Keep fighting the good fight." Signed with Much Love, Ashia Manning

Robert Cohen was born on July 9, 1982 and although he was diagnosed with cerebral palsy only a year later, he never let that stop him from achieving his goals.

Cohen is a native of Savannah, Georgia. He was educated in Chatham County Public Schools and received his high school diploma in 2001. He continued his education at Savannah State University from 2001 through 2005 when he earned his of Bachelor's in Science in Sociology and minored in Psychology.

Robert Cohen was brought up in the historic First African Baptist Church in Downtown Savannah. At the age of 23, Cohen received his license in Ministry. He is now a member of First Jerusalem Baptist Church on the Westside of Savannah near Liberty City where he serves on the Greeter's Ministry and he also assists in Group Ministering.

Cohen is currently a member of the Brandon Heart's International Church. Where he does motivational speaking, prayer, and devotional services.

In 2007, he started volunteering with the Chatham Savannah Citizen's Advocacy and joined the Board of Directors. He has been an active member for the past three years and served as Chairman of the Board of Directors.

Robert Cohen has worked for the City of Savannah for the past 12 years as a summer camp youth counselor where he counseled children aged 6-13 on many topics from drug and alcohol prevention to the importance of staying in school.

Cohen has done lots of volunteer work, such as working with the Therapeutic Program at the John S. Delaware recreation center in 2006, working for Goodwill as a mentor in 2010 and working at Memorial Health University as an out-patient escort in 2011.

In November of 2010, Cohen published his first book, "Joys, Fears and Tears" which is a compilation of his life experiences in the form of poetry. He expresses how he feels about situations that occurred in his lifetime; from living with cerebral palsy, to different family situations, to relationships with friends and female acquaintances.

In November of 2013, Cohen published, "Inspiration: Physically Challenged but Mentally Determined," a book written to inspire others that with the help of God, hard work and dedication, anything is possible.

In December of 2013, Cohen published, "Faceoff: Men vs. Women Needs, Wants, & Desires." This book discusses relationships and situations that couples go through in these relationships.

Finally, he has most recently written *Soul of Love* in December of 2015. It is a collection of love poems that discuss love in its different forms.

In March of 2015, Cohen became ordained as a licensed Minister.

Jumping Through Life's Hurdles With A Smile: You Can Only Play The Hand You're Dealt

By: Robert Cohen

Jumping Through Life's Hurdles With A Smile

X

R.E.C.

By Robert Elliott Cohen
Robert E. Cohen

Content

Preface

Perseverance is each of your ability to move from one level of your life to another. Much like all of you, I also had obstacles to persevere in life. Being born with a development disability called cerebral palsy sometimes made it hard for me to see myself persevering to the next level in my life because I was worried about how people would perceive me. I didn't want people to see the wheelchair and have preconceived notions about my learning ability simply because I had a physical disability. But with hard work, dedication, and the help given to me by God, my family, and my friends enabled me to preserver through the obstacles that I felt held me back the most. Like me, you all must also apply hard work and dedication in your life to preserver and reach the next level. I believe anything is possible. On March 28, 2015, I became an 'ordained minister. For some, that would mean continuing school to get a higher degree and for others that means being dedicated to a job search until finding what it is you want to do in life. "Whichever path you choose, do your best and persevere to the next level of your life." –Robert Cohen 2016

Robert Cohen is the son of Robert and the late Gladys Cohen. Born on July 9, 1982, I was born with a physical condition called Cerebral palsy which is a brain effect that causes a person not to be physical walk. I was diagnosed with it when I was one years old.

This explains the reason why I am in a wheelchair. My physical condition has never hindered my ability to function in society. I have always been an outgoing and outspoken person that has never let my physical limitations prevent me from being what I choose to be in life.

I have the disability the disability doesn't have me and the disability will never define me or what I choose to be in society. I was educated in Chatham County Public School System. During my tenure in school, I had to deal with a lot I had to overcome a lot of obstacles from getting to know people and not have them be fearful of me because of my appearance.

This task will sometimes a difficult one because some people didn't understand my condition and why I was in a wheelchair and therefore they couldn't see past the wheelchair until I was able to actually sit down and explain to them that my appearance was just different and I had to go through the same obstacles they went to so I had to talk to them and explain so that they wouldn't be ignorant about people that maybe different from them.

As I went through school, certain things were difficult for me to accomplish because of my physical limitations. Never the less, I never made excuses for why I couldn't excel with my education. However, I needed ascendance with certain things in school. It was never a problem for me because of the ascendance I was able to get from my family and my strong support system.

I am a very determined black male who has worked very diligently to accomplish life. I was educated in the Chatham County Public School system for the duration of my schooling. I graduated from high school with a regular college prep-diploma from Johnson High School, June 2001. In August 2001, I began my college career at Savannah State University. As a black male living with the developmental disability can sometimes be a very difficult thing to do.

Having to deal with several different challenges such as not being able to dress myself, feeding myself, or physically writing making each obstacle a little more different from the last, but with the help of god my family and friends makes this a lot easier for me to accomplish. My personality gives me the strength and ability to not strength and ability to not sit around and feel bad for myself. I rather get up and get out because there is too much life for me to sit around and feel sorry for myself.

As a black living in today's society can be a very difficult and interesting experience for someone with a physical disability because they are always being challenged with the struggles of daily life. As I continue to live every day to the fullest I have always remember, just because I may not physically be able to do much for myself I always find ways to yet overcome the struggles of everyday life because of my strong will and outgoing personality.

It is never difficult for me to help me with things I need help with. I am very grateful for my friends and family and for everything that they help me with and have allowed me to achieve up to this point. Currently I am a part of several different groups in the Savannah community. One is being Savannah Chatham Community Advocacy Organization, where I serve as chairman.

In this road I have several different responsibilities. One of which is organizing board orientations for incoming board members as well as overseeing the monthly board meeting, delegating responsibilities to the members of the board and making difficult decisions in the best interest of the board.

For those who do not know, cerebral palsy is the name for a condition in which brain damage has disrupted normal muscle functioning.

Spastic quadriplegia affects the entire body. Spastic refers to the muscle stiffness which accompanies the condition. Quadri—comes from the Latin for four; it means that all four quadrants of the body are affected by spastic quadriplegia. Plegia comes from the Greek term for a form of paralysis.

This medical condition I have has a large impact on my lifestyle. There are so many challenges I face from day to day. In spite of it all, I have become very accomplished. I am successful because I have learned to be persistent. "No matter what you face you can do anything if you put your mind."

I want my experiences to help others achieve their goals. I've spoken into peoples' lives. I believe that you can do anything you put your mind because Christ has given all of us a measure of strength to use for his Glory. We should be doing that to the best of the ability Gods given us. Philippians 4:13 says: "I can do all things through Christ who strengthens me" New King James Version

New Living Translation says: "For I can do everything through Christ, who gives me strength." Also, 1 Corinthians 15:58 New International Version says; "Therefore, my dear brothers and sisters, stand firm. Lord, because you know that your labor in the Lord is not in vain. New King James Version says; "Therefore, my dear brothers and sister stand firm. Let nothing move you. Always give yourselves fully to the work of the Lord is not in vain."

Life

Sometimes deals us difficult circumstances
Some are not in our control
Such as being born with a developmental disability
Or attempting to pursue a career
Where you feel like you're serving a purpose to society
The storms can honestly beat you down to the ground;
If you aren't anchored in God 100%
Your mind will play kinds of tricks on you,
Making you believe all kinds of things
That are not even true
Sometimes life can be a very difficult thing to deal with
When you're in a certain situation

CHAPTER 1
The Birth of a Champion

Birth
Robert E. Cohen

A birth is a very glorious experience that will assist you in having a more joyful life with a lot of high points that you enjoy after the birth has occurred. Another thing about a birth is there are a lot of responsibilities to be taken care of. A lot of teenagers make the mistake of letting a birth happen before they are really prepared to care for a newborn. They are stuck without anyone to help them. So never make a birth before you are prepared.

CHAPTER 2

The Challenges of Life Struggles

Challenges

In life everyone will encounter challenges at some point

When challenges arise, it's not the challenge that we but
it's how we handle the challenge that is important

It is important to handle the challenge with careful consideration
of everything and everyone involved in the challenge to ensure
that it is handled the best way possible for all people

Challenges never inform you of when they're coming,
they just come and you have to handle it the best way
you know how, with the best judgment you can

Don't get discouraged because the challenge will not
last but a little while and at the end you will smile

Sometimes it takes someone in different situation for people who are
able bodied to see how blessed they are because they don't always want

or have the drive to get up and do what they need to do. My books came from life experiences and the desire to express my point of view. I see life in a different perspective than others. Writing my books has been an outlet for me. It's allowed me to release undo pressure.

I have learned to be persistent because I have to get assistance for getting dressed, bathed, and grooming. In school I had to have assistance with writing. I found people that would write notes for me. Then, there were some times when school became somewhat more challenging on certain occasions than others.

Schoolwork was difficult because note takers were not always available. I always to try to stay on top my schoolwork in spite of the obstacles, I faced. I would always to try to put my best foot forward. Even though sometimes there a lot of adversity taking place in my life. I am able to verbalize and explain how to do to what I need done. It is important for me to use my voice. I want others to be successful too.

What kept me going was that I knew that I could inspire others. It was and still is my motivation for serving as the chairman of the board of directors for Chatham Savannah Citizen Advocacy, assisting with Greeters Ministry, Group Ministry, summer camp youth counselor, mentoring, and volunteering as an escort for Memorial Health University's out-patients.

Human Mental Frustration

Human mental frustration comes when life starts to get you down and you seem to feel like there's no way out. What you must do during these times is remember that God is always there for you and He will always help you out with anything we perceive to be a problem.

Just pray, Keep God first and He will always be there for you.

When you're mentally frustrated God can always bless you because when you're at your weakest point, He can bring you out of your struggles so He can bless you abundantly.

CHAPTER 3
The Crowning of a King

Smile

When you smile

It takes a lot of the pain away

When you smile

It makes things go along smoother

When you smile

You can tend to get more done in the run of a day

When you smile

You have a lot more happiness in your life

So always try to smile in everything you do

I was a well-known guy in high school. Everyone knew me because I always made my presence felt. Everyone was always so willing and engaged to help. It's never was a problem to get what I needed. My senior, I was nominated for the homecoming king position by Ivan Smith. He has always been a good friend to me. We had several classes together while in high school. One class we shared was 11th grade English. He was major part in me deciding to run for homecoming king. The week of homecoming, I did several things to prepare. I set up posters around the school. It was important to stay organized. The Thursday before homecoming, all the contestants had to stay after class. We rehearsed, so that each of us would know where to be on the football field for the game. On that Friday, there was a pep rally for us. After school, I went home put on my tuxedo and waited. The game wasn't until 7:30pm. My classmate Monique Chapman sang the national anthem as an opener for the game. Five minutes before the second quarter ended, the homecoming court had to line up for processional. I was positioned between the forty and fifty-yard line on the football field. At that point, I was really nervous.

I watched as the game went on. Once the buzzer sounded to end the second quarter, we all went down to the field and took our places. They announced the second runner up of first who was Mark Beamon. The first runner was Robert Reddick. After that a hush went over the crowd as they got ready to announce the winner. I didn't realize at the time it was me, but I was anxious. Finally, they announced my name as the being the homecoming king Johnson High school. I received a crown from my classmate who was chosen the year before; his name is Melvin Brown with a huge smile on my face. In that moment people were taking lots of pictures and screaming my name. I was relieved because the nervousness was finally gone.

Robert Cohen and Shaqueshia Gibson - 2000

Me at my 2001 high school homecoming
being crowned homecoming King!

PLEASE MEET:
ROBERT COHEN

'God wouldn't let me give up'

By Jenel Few
912.652.0325 • jenel.few@savannahnow.com

If you happen to meet Robert Cohen, consid
yourself lucky.

"I try to be encouraging," Cohen said. "People look
at me and see what I have to go through to get where
I'm going and if nothing else, that is encouraging."

Robert, now 23, was not supposed to make it beyond
his first week of life.

He and twin sister Robin were born 12 weeks early.
Robin came through just fine. Robert, who weighed
just two pounds at birth, had a much rougher time
and spent his first two weeks on a ventilator.

"His second day of life the doctors gave up on him.
They told me he wasn't going to make it," said his
mother Gladys Cohen. "Two weeks later, they said
he'd probably make it but he would be blind, deaf or
mentally retarded."

Robert is none of those things.

His parents enrolled him in public school when he
was five and they demanded placement in regular
classes.

His condition left him reliant on a wheelchair. His
speech is slightly impaired and he must use a com-

see **COHEN**, page **4B**

Cohen

Continued from page 1B

puter because he is unable to write.

But it's nothing Robert couldn't work around.

"He has physical limitations," his mother said. "But no mental limitations."

In fourth grade Robert wrote a poem depicting his life and outlook. It was published in Highlights Magazine:

"I have wheels and I can roll.
I may never ride a bike
But I can go."

A Johnson High School alum, he was crowned homecoming king his senior year and earned a HOPE Scholarship.

When it came time to cross the stage and accept his high school diploma, the principal made arrangements to hand Robert his diploma while the other students made their way up the stairs to the platform.

"Wrong answer!," his mother said. "I told him you better find some lifts from somewhere."

And on Dec. 9, during Savannah State University's winter graduation, somebody found another lift.

Robert used it to cross the stage at Tiger Arena and accept his Bachelor of Science degree in Sociology.

"It was very important for me to cross the stage like everybody else," Robert said. "I met the same academic requirements."

Robert's classmates say he is an inspiration.

His professors say his attitude and determination were incredible.

Richard Burkhart/Savannah Morning News

Robert Cohen is congratulated by Joseph "Pete" Silver, Vice President of Academic Services, after receiving his diploma during Savannah State University's winter commencement ceremony.

But Robert, who is preparing to become a Baptist preacher before pursuing a master's degree in counseling, gives the credit to a much higher power.

He preached his second ser-mon, about the power of prayer, at First African Baptist Church the day after graduation.

"Faith in God got me all the way to college and God wouldn't let me give up," Robert said.

CHAPTER 4
Fighting Struggles

Fighting Struggles can sometimes be a very difficult task to accomplish in today's society. There are many different things going on in our cities, states and countries that people are consumed with their own issues. No one really has time to listen to the struggles of other people in their networks. While this is understandable at some point in time, you just have to take your mind off your own problems and make time to listen to someone else. You never know that a person is going through in their personal life and the fact that you take a few minutes out of your day to help them, may be all they need to get pass the struggle they're going through at that time. If you ever find yourself in a position where you can be a blessing to someone else's situation, always do what you can to assist them.

In my daily walk, this is something that I find myself engaged in quite often because in my circle, my friends, family and others look to me for advice to help them with their issue. It tells me that they respect me and my opinion and they appreciate me being there for them. In life you always have to be very careful of how you treat people. You never know where your blessing may come from and how you impact someone's life by your words and actions.

Robert Cohen

CHAPTER 5
Opportunities

Our hearts are filled with lots of simple treasures, some of which we as human beings may never discover. In life, we don't take full advantage of the opportunities life presents us. Life is filled with chances and possibilities of all sorts. We as people are living in a society where people must compete for their opportunity therefore if you are blessed. To receive an opportunity, take full advantage of the opportunity because you could lose it.

In life, we never know what opportunities God will bless us with. Some of those opportunities may include the people we meet on a day to day basis. This person is a very sweet and kind-hearted person who I'm glad I've had the pleasure of meeting and knowing. I pray God continue to bless me with opportunities to meet the people that will transform my life and help me to become the man that God meant for me to be. There are a lot of opportunities that are presented to us that we miss for one reason or another, such as job opportunities that will hopefully get us to where we want to be in life and help us see our full potential.

In 2007, I started volunteering with the Chatham Savannah Citizen's Advocacy and joined the Board of Directors. I served as a Board Chair for the last two years of my matriculation. He has been an active member from 2007-2015 and in 2012 served as Chairman of the Board of Directors. In this position, I lead all of the meetings for the span of two years. This was a very challenging task to achieve because at my first meeting as Board Chair, we lost a Board Member so it took a lot of transitioning, time and effort to get back on track. I also had to lead the annual Citizens Advocacy Covered Dish Dinner.

During the last year of my term as Chairman of the
Board of Chatham Savannah Citizen Advocacy

Struggles of Everyday Life for an Individual with a Disability

Living with a disability can very challenging at times, because you have to deal with uninformed people, who don't necessarily understand how to respond to people with different conditions. I have had two separate incidents in the past month that proves this point to be very true. Both of these incidents involved ADA title III violations.

September 12, 2019

I'm writing you this email to tell you about a situation that happened today on my first ride. I was getting off the bus getting dropped off to my first destination and I asked the operator could she please open the door to the business for me.

She went into a spat about me not speaking to her when I get on the bus but the reason why I don't speak to her is because she acts like she has an attitude every time she sees me so I'd rather not speak to her to protect my feelings. I like to avoid confrontation.

To make a long story short she didn't open the door for me and this is an issue for me because I'm in a wheelchair and I have slight asthma problems. She pulled off without opening the door which left me out in the heat for over 30 minutes.

Just because I don't speak to her shouldn't affect how she does her job.

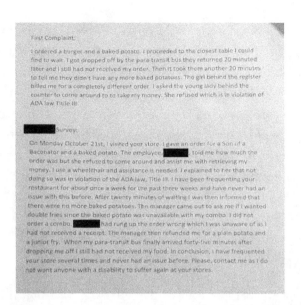

First Complaint:

I ordered a burger and a baked potato. I proceeded to the closest table I could find to wait. I got dropped off by the para-transit bus they returned 20 minutes later and I still had not received my order. Then it took them another 20 minutes to tell me they didn't have any more baked potatoes. The girl behind the register billed me for a completely different order. I asked the young lady behind the counter to come around to to take my money. She refused which is in violation of ADA law Title III.

████████ Survey:

On Monday October 21st, I visited your store. I gave an order for a Son of a Baconator and a baked potato. The employee, ████████, told me how much the order was but she refused to come around and assist me with retrieving my money. I use a wheelchair and assistance is needed. I explained to her that not doing so was in violation of the ADA law, Title III. I have been frequenting your restaurant for about once a week for the past three weeks and have never had an issue with this before. After twenty minutes of waiting I was then informed that there were no more baked potatoes. The manager came out to ask me if I wanted double fries since the baked potato was unavailable with my combo. I did not order a combo. ████████ had rung up the order wrong which I was unaware of as I had not received a receipt. The manager then refunded me for a plain potato and a junior fry. When my para-transit bus finally arrived forty-five minutes after dropping me off I still had not received my food. In conclusion, I have frequented your store several times and never had an issue before. Please, contact me as I do not want anyone with a disability to suffer again at your stores.

Good afternoon, I really need to talk to you about the matter I emailed you about a couple weeks ago. Could you please get back with me at your earliest convenience? And because of the matter that happens on September 12 with (bus driver), I requested not to be placed on vehicle 1806 anymore. And I was placed on manifest on Monday afternoon for my 4 o clock trip going from 4700 waters to 7400 Abercorn. Once again, she went into another spat about me not speaking to her. I am really tired of her and her attitude and I would really rather not be placed on her manifest. Therefore, the company can avoid legal action from me, I would strongly suggest that you get this email to the proper people. I'm sick of dealing with these female drivers and their attitude and I'm getting ready to take legal action and also with this bus driver because of the situation that happened with her on November 12, could you please talk to the the schedulist because they are really getting on my nerves because they are paid to help us and if they don't want these kind of jobs, they don't need to apply for them. I just got off bus 16 with (bus driver) she did 2 things wrong she tied me down and told me to move my chair and I said she needed to untie me.. when she dropped me off at she dropped me off in the grass and not in the proper place..

On Saturday on bus number, 1611 operator asked me how I was paying for my trip. I replied that I was paying with cash and she gave me a funny look and said get it out with a nasty attitude. It would seem to me that if you look at me you can tell I have problems using my hands so for her to come out and say that was rude and disrespectful. This is the third email I have sent about this operator in the past 3 weeks. I am sick of her inconsiderate behavior towards me and I am sure she's doing it to other people.

Would it be possible for me to pay round trip to my first driver for the day and can I not be on her schedule for pick up at all because it is going to get ugly.

Last Tuesday 10/15/19 on my last pick up from 307 mall Blvd to 6947 key Street the driver arrived at 3:07pm and I was trying to get loaded on the bus and the operator left the wheelchair lift up so I can get on the bus and as I was backing in I guess I was moving too slow for him because I had to readjust my chair a couple times and I guess his patients got short and he told me since I didn't want back on the bus I could get off and he could go about his business please check tape on bus 1811 from Tuesday night and please talk to this operator this is my second incident with him in the past two weeks his name is (bus driver name)

On Friday 10/20/19 on my 2:06pm ride from Savannah State bookstore the driver loaded me on the wrong side of the street the bus was facing wrong way to load me. She was wondering why I was frustrated but you have to load the wheelchair on the curbside of the street. This was the incorrect way to load a wheelchair onto the vehicle also very dangerous please check the tape from bus 1828 from Friday afternoon at 2:00pm

Good Afternoon, I'm about to tell you about the second incident that happened last night with the same driver from November 12th. Last night on November 22nd, I had a 7 o'clock appointment from the mall to Johnson high school at 3012 sunset blvd she asked me if I was going to 8410 Waters Ave at the beginning, I told her I wasn't sure at the cause I was going to get my dad to go there for me. Upon arriving at the school, the driver did not want to let me off the bus because the security guard told her that game was sold out. I told her to go ahead and let me off the bus because I wasn't taking up a seat in the gym so they should let me in...which they did. This caused her to get an even worst attitude because she already didn't want to do her job to begin with. She caused me to get out of creator just a little bit. Full disclosure I did tell her "shut up and stay out my business", because she seemed to forget she's there to do a job. And like I said in my previous email if you don't have compassion for people with special needs you don't need to be doing this job. Full disclosure I'm sick of operator. I rather not ride with her. Please check the video tape on the bus she was driving last night this will confirm everything that happened last night.

Good afternoon, I really need to talk to you about the matter I emailed you about a couple weeks ago. Could you please get back with me at your earliest convenience? And because of the matter that happens on September 12 with the operator. I requested not to be placed on vehicle 1806 anymore. And I was placed on manifest on Monday afternoon for my 4 o clock trip going from 4700 waters to 7400 Abercorn. Once again she went into another spat about me not speaking to her. I'm really tired of her and her attitude and I would really rather not be placed on her manifest. And so the company can avoid legal action from me, I would strongly suggest that you get this email to the proper people. I'm sick of dealing with these female drivers and their attitude because of the situation that happened with her on November 12. Could you please talk to the person that makes the schedule because they are really getting on my nerves because they are paid to help us and if they don't want these kind of jobs, they don't need to apply for them? I just got off bus 16 with the operator she did 2 things wrong she tied me down and told me to move my chair and I said she needed to untie me. When she dropped me off at she dropped me off in the grass and not in the proper place.

Good afternoon, I'm writing to tell you about two separate incidents that happened with the same operator on two different occasions. Let's begin with the first incident on November 12th, I had scheduled an appointment at 7 o'clock that evening to 3219 College Street from 7804 Abercorn. The vehicle number was 1613, she loaded me up on the bus, and I told her I wasn't going to checkers when she picked me up at 10 o'clock. By the time she came back, I contacted my dad. My dad informed me there's nothing to eat at the house, so I needed to keep my ride to go to checkers. When I got on the bus and told her I needed to go to checkers. The driver told me she wasn't going to take me to checkers because I said I wasn't going to go earlier but we was already close to the destination. However, when she came back to get me, checkers was still on manifest so technically she can't tell me she can't take me because it was still on her manifest. When I told her, she caught an attitude and said "let me take you to checkers because I know what you're trying to do. If you not out by the time pick up, I'm gone leave you." The whole incident started because she had attitude about me telling her I wasn't going to checkers when she pick me back up. But in my opinion she wants a pay check but don't want to do the work, if you don't have a care and compassion for people you don't need to be working that job.

Good evening, I'm writing you this email to inform you of a situation that took place last Friday on vehicle 1702. I was getting picked from the 7804 Abercorn going to 1722 Habersham St. and upon getting in the vehicle, the operator got out of the van came around the van opened the door and the doors of passenger's seat were halfway back. When I asked her to lift the seats she took her downtime about it. When I entered into the vehicle she asked if her if was I able to move my wheel chair around and I informed her that I wouldn't be able to because there was another passenger in the van. She closed the sliding doors without the restraining my wheelchair to keep it firm moving while on the road. The excuse that she will use is that there was another passenger on the van and I wasn't able to turn the wheelchair. However, that would not prevent her from restraining my wheelchair because it doesn't matter how I go into the vehicle, you can still put down restraints on my

Robert Cohen

wheelchair on both sides, it doesn't matter how I am positioned. This a very dangerous hazard for me because the suspension of my chair is messed up so the wheel chair will move even if it's tied down so if it is tied down it will love even worse. This is the about the 4th incident I've had with this operator in the past month. As I explained to you in the previous emails and on the phone, I told you it was going to get very ugly. This will soon turn into a lawsuit. I strongly suggest that you talk to her and explain to her that under the disability act title 3 it is against the law to place a wheelchair in a vehicle without tying it down. Technically I am entitled to pursue a lawsuit. When I ride on this vehicle I must be tied down because if something happens to me, Chatham area transit will be responsible.

Good evening I am writing to inform you of an incident that happened on January 23, 2020 on my 7:15 ride from 7804 Abercorn to 3219 college Street. I got on the bus with the operator. I made two attempts to hand her my fair once before I got on and one after she tied me down. She refused to take it and she was riding one of the dollars fell on the floor. When got ready to unload me she told me I better figure out a way to pick it up from off the floor. Then she told me that she will tell you all that I paid a dollar when I gave two one just feel on the floor. This is the fifth incident I've had and I'm not happy. If y'all don't stop putting her on the schedule I will take it to illegal matters and have the issue handle. This is against ADA laws title three. I sincerely hope you all take this seriously.

Good afternoon, on Friday (1/24/20) I had a trip scheduled from 7804 Abercorn to 1722 Habersham Street; however, I got a call yesterday morning that the Habersham street event was cancelled. I, in turn, call center supervisor, to inform her that event had been cancelled and that I would possibly need to rearrange my pick-up. She called me back about 5 minutes later and told me that she wouldn't be able to make any changes. She said that 2 drivers had called out yesterday, but she gave me the option to get the regular city bus which I had attempted to do leaving from 7804 Abercorn to 8410 Waters Ave. when the 6 cross town bus arrived. The operator informed me that he had already passed that stop and that he wasn't going to be stopping there again because he was on his last trip and was going to the garage for the night. The operator then called the office on his cell phone to him know what was going on and that I needed to be picked up because he was going on the other end of town and didn't want me riding with him all night. I informed the dispatcher of what I needed her to do because I was originally scheduled to go from 8410 Waters ave to go home at 11:15 pm. But they changed my pickup for the day, so the lady in the call center advised me to catch the 8:35, the 6 cross town, on Hodgson Memorial and Mall Blvd. and then to 8410 Waters Ave. By the time he called me back, he had already made it to 14045 Abercorn. The dispatcher finally called me back and asked me where I was going to get off the bus at. I told her at 14045 Abercorn is where I would get off. She said "okay, I'm going to send the driver to that location." So when I said if the driver could drop me off at 8410 Waters Ave, the driver said no because I wasn't where I was supposed to be. But I was supposed to be there initially, but it wasn't my fault that I was given the wrong time at the call center. But the dispatcher made it seem like it was my fault and I was only doing what call center lead told me to do earlier that day because they weren't able to reschedule my ride. So, it wasn't my fault that I wasn't going to be at 8410 Waters Ave. There is a problem with the situation that happened last night: I am disabled and I think I did a very good job of attempted to get to where I was trying to be to catch the regular bus and I should not have to be penalized because I was given the wrong information by the call center about the times. Her not allowing me to go to 8410 Waters Ave to get something to eat when it was scheduled properly and just because she had to send the driver to 14045 Abercorn. I should not have to be penalized and that's the second time in 3 weeks that she has done that and she is the only dispatcher that treats me like everything is my fault when it really isn't. And she should understand because she used to be a driver and she should realize this because she should know that things get hectic out on the streets. Would you please kindly address this situation with her because I or anybody else doesn't deserve to be treated like this because we have rights too.

Robert Cohen

CHAPTER 6
A Distant Relationship

Disappointment and Hurt

Robert E Cohen

In my heart lately all that I can feel is disappointment and hurt. The reason for it, well honestly, there is no reason except for the fact that I am physically disabled which limits the things that I am able to do independently. This is a serious concern for me because some things that I need are very crucial for daily living. When I ask someone in my family for something they are slow about getting it for me and it makes me feel as if I am talking to a brick wall. That is what makes me feel all this disappointment and hurt in my heart which at some point is going to transform into just plain anger. Before I end up directing my emotions in the wrong place I try to avoid saying anything to anybody. I don't want to appear to be a heartless person because I am not that type of person. It's very unfortunate that I get treated better by outsiders than my own family. This is where majority of my disappointment and hurt comes from.

The Hurt in My Heart

Robert E Cohen

The hurt in my heart is very painful because sometimes I feel as if no one is interested in what I have to say. Even though I don't show it all the time someone ignores me I feel hurt. I am really having trouble trying to figure out how people could be so cold hearted and still sleep comfortably at night knowing what they are not treating me the way that I deserve to be treated. Certain individuals think just because I am not able to do certain things for myself that gives them the right to disrespect me and expect me to just sit there and take it with no response. As I try to do that it does not always work because I find it hard to be humble when someone is disrespecting me for no apparent reason.

Example: When I ask for something to drink they say wait a minute and it may be another twenty minutes before I get it. I have to ask repeatedly because either they forget or they just don't care. Now I should not feel that way but how cannot when that is what's really going on.

The Mental Death

Robert E. Cohen

When someone dies mentally it does not mean that they are brain dead, it simply means that they may be experiencing something that has their attention so diverted that it may affect their everyday performance in achieving the tasks they have to deal with successfully. If your mind is preoccupied there is a great possibility that you won't be at one hundred percent.

CHAPTER 7
My Grief After Loss of a Good Friend

Homeboy

Robert E Cohen
Dedication: The Late Travis Williams

Homeboy you're in Heaven now and since your departure I have experienced a certain amount of difficulty dealing with your death. I really don't understand why. You have been gone for more than a year but when the accident first happened it was not as much of a conflict as it has been the past three months. For the past three months I have not been able to really focus on anything except you because when you died it really tore me apart.

Rest In Peace Homeboy

The Lost Homeboy

Robert Cohen
Dedication: The Late Travis Williams

The loss of a homeboy can be a very difficult thing to deal with because you never know when it will hit you that the person is actually gone and you will never see that person again. When it does hit and you realize that all the good times that you and that person had are over. It may take a while for you to come to the realization but when it does it will hurt and may take months, even years, to overcome this very painful obstacle. My homeboy has been dead for over a year and I have yet to overcome his death.

Brother

Robert E. Cohen
Dedication: The Late Travis Williams

Brother, you left earth to go be with your Father in Heaven. When you first died it did not cause me as much of a conflict as it is right now because there is not a day that passes that you don't cross my mind. Brother, you not only left me but you left an empty space in my heart reserved for memories of you. Oh how I miss you and adore you and hope to see you again someday.

CHAPTER 8
Inspirational Poems

Best of Friends
By: Robert E. Cohen

When people meet each other, they're hoping that they become the best of friends and hopefully they can stay the best of friends forever.

The person that is my best friend in the world has a beautiful personality and someone who I care about deeply.

I pray every night that we remain friends forever and for life and that nothing will come between us that will stop our friendship. I pray God bless us and keep at all times and keep us in His loving arms of protection.

I hope you doing ok and know I'm always thinking of you.

You know you have a special place in my heart and always will so always remember that no matter what.

The Misunderstood Godly Man

Have you ever felt misunderstood? Like life was passing you by? And you sit in a room trying to figure out why God doesn't hear what you think? No matter what you do, it never feels like enough. It seems like you're getting nothing out of your endeavors. Because, Truly, this is how I've been feeling. I know I am God's child. I believe his word and I believe he has a purpose and a plan for my life. However, the process seems as if it's at a standstill. And what don't want to do, is give up on God! I strive to do everything I can to be good to people, but it seems as if no one is hearing my cry for help in the physical. I know God hears me, but I feel like I need somebody in the physical world to help me work through the discouraging moments in my life. I refuse to give the devil any authority in my life. He will cause me to be in this phase of my life longer than God intends. Truly there are times that I feel misunderstood and I need God to help me through it.

Dear God I pray your guidance over my life right now! Help me to understand your word. I need people in my life that will help me get back to your word.

The Real Friend
Rita Spear
Jan. 16th, 2017

The real friend is someone who has a willing spirit, and a great heart. Someone in which you can confide in and not have to worry about it going any further than the two of you. It's the great feeling of knowing you can brighten this person's day with a smile or an encouraging word. I want you know I'm the real friend and no matter what happens I'll be there for you. You never have to hesitate to talk to me, I love our friendship, but I've grown to love the person you are more.

Confusion of Love

In love there are several variables that you have to deal with; some of them being difficult such as getting to know one another and making sure you both are compatible to one another. Without doing this it is even harder to develop a relationship. People sometimes seem to forget about the face to face in a relationship because everything is more geared toward social media and technology. No one takes the time to go out on dates, getting to know each other and really get the understanding of what getting to know a person is. Going out on dates, going to the movies, taking the time to spend quality time with one another. This way, the two of you can get familiar with one another before the intimacy factor comes into play. This would avoid a lot of not knowing one another and just jumping into bed with one another before you really get to know one another the way you should.

Robert Cohen

Love Hurts

Why is real true unconditional love so distant in my life? I give all of me
to love and my heart constantly gets destroyed. Love is not
suppose to feel this way. Love should not disappoint me constantly,
unfortunately, it does. Unconditional love has no limits and no
boundaries. Oh what I would do for love if only the ones I love
appreciated it! Real True Unconditional Love is few and far between in
my life currently.

Storms

Storms can sometimes be very difficult things to deal with, but there are also different types of storms we have to deal with in our life. Some storms we deal with are hard and physical storms like the storm with the weather, and other storms are mental storms we deal with in everyday life such as Hurricane Matthew. Hurricane Matthew was a physical storm that did a lot of physical damage to the city of Savannah. We as people sometimes don't realize how blessed we are to be living in the world that we live in because there are third world countries such as Haiti that are suffering that don't have much to start with and the little that they did have, they lost most of it to Hurricane Matthew.

Now there is another type of storm that I want to deal with; the mental storm of everyday life that we have to deal with there are certain storms in our life that we just can't get around and there are certain storms that God takes us through to get us where he feels like we need to be so that he can bless us and we must take heed to his Word. But, God will not infringe on your free will so it's up to you to choose him and all he will do is gently call you and if you don't heed his message then he'll give you fair warning and most times he will give you more than one warning. It just takes the ones who answer longer to answer because they don't fully understand the benefits of having a relationship with God. The people that don't answer do not understand the days and times that we are living in and how important having a relationship with God is. It takes time for them to have a relationship with God, so always be careful in what you do and make sure what you do is done in love and because you want to. God won't force you to do anything, and you shouldn't let anyone else push you to do anything either.

When I started school, my relationship with my mom started shifting to something really awkward. From the time I was diagnosed with cerebral palsy up until currently, I feel that she has resentment towards me and hasn't show much tender, love, and care. This really bothered me. I don't feel connected in that area of my life. I feel like some of my issues with the opposite sex have come from it. It's definitely played a role.

She doesn't do much for me as far as the physical aspect. I'm hurt by that and disappointed. The fact that my condition is caused by a birth defect, I think our relationship is strained there's an underlying issues. I think my mother has never expressed. She might be internalizing. I wish that she will tell me how she feels. I want to open up. So I can at least attempt to figure out how to deal with it. I wish I knew what was going on. If I knew I make an attempt to fix it. The baggage that I carry from my mom has some effect on the relationship we have. I feel like I can't trust giving my heart to the fairer sex, because of the difficult variables in my relationship with my mom.

Being that I did have a rough patch in the relationship with my mom, it has made me realize not to set expectation to high when it comes to getting assistance. I learned to be more cautious when it comes relationships with the opposite sex.

I know it won't always be there, just like it wasn't always there while, I was in school. As time moves forward I'm figuring what the best path for my life is. Even though, it seems to be a serious, dark, cloud over my life.

Nevertheless, I will continue to keep my spirits up and stay encouraged because I know at times, my smile and personality is the only thing that keeps me going. I wouldn't want to deprive anybody else of their blessing because I'm not 100% myself.

As time moves forward I'm finding it a lot easier to deal with that relationship. It's allowing me to have an easier time dealing with the other relationships that I have, because that relationship has gotten better. However, sometimes I find myself going back to that dark place.

I desire a relationship but, I have not found the one yet. In finding a relationship it's always a difficult thing to do because there are so many different factors that have to be examined. First, you have to seek God. Tell him exactly what you want and wait until He guides you to that person, or that person to you.

You have to first of all, know what you want out of a relationship. Then seek God, wait for him to answer to your question. At times people's emotion can overshadow their judgment. This is why a lot of people get hurt in relationships. It's because people don't think clearly when they're going by their head and not their heart. Once you get your heart on one accord, stop letting the devil get in your mind.

Angel

Monday, May 8, 2017

To: Tierra Kirk

Sometimes God places people in our lives for unknown reasons; reasons that we don't understand, reasons that God doesn't reveal to us until later on in life. An angel always looks out for you, always is there for you, and always protects you, even though you may not know they're looking out for you. God always has a ram in your bush for anything you go through. My angel has been there for me through everything; throughout the past few months and I really appreciate her.

Behind Closed Doors

Monday, May 8, 2017

Behind closed doors, no one knows the pain you go thru, no one knows the suffering you deal with, no one knows what really goes on with you. Behind closed doors, people think just because you have a smile on your face everything is all beautiful and perfect. But most times this is not the case, especially in my life, because right now I'm going through so much turmoil and pain. But with the people in my life and with my mental struggle I endure, people wouldn't understand. Even if I told them what I was going through they wouldn't get it. Just because you see the people around you with a smile on their face, doesn't mean they are not going through something. Don't take it for granted that they may be going through something or may be having problems. Because it's always somebody out here who has problems and we should always try to help them with difficulties as much as we can.

Robert Cohen

Why I Write

July 11, 2017

I write to express the internal-emotional feelings of my heart.

I write to express to the world about how I feel about what goes on in my life.

I write to release the mental; and emotional pain that I feel at times, when I feel like no one understands.

I write to express my freedom of speech, in my very own way.

I write to show the world that even with a disability I can do what I need to do and still be successful; despite the obstacles I face on a daily basis.

I write because I want to show those on the internet and social media that I am here, and even despite my situation they shouldn't be worried.

This is because I am made a prosperous person by the grace of god and he blessed me so I can bless others around me.

I write to give peace and hope to this distressed world that we live in.

Emotional Hurt

August 16, 2017

When a person experience emotional hurt it can come from several different life experiences. Some people experience emotional hurt by going through a breakup. Some people are not use to dealing with an emotional breakup, emotional there is lot of emotions hurt that comes with it. This happens more so people that are just starting to find love and not use of handling variables that go along with it such as getting to learn the person so the relationship goes sour. You have to prepare yourself for the challenges that life will bring you on the day by day basis. Do not allow hurt to get you to the point you feel like you can't move forward with life. Just pray about it and keep it moving. Because at the end of the day life must go on.

Love vs. Lust
August 16, 2017

Love is a serious emotional feeling that involves two hearts getting to know one another

This is very difficult task to deal with because when two people meet there two variables examine when getting to know one another. First, examine your personal relationship with God. Be sure that God has justified you to go out and look for a relationship, if he hasn't you must wait for his directions. He has for you, if not he will give you several signs.

The lust factor is very strange because people tend to confuse lust with love. Lust is strong feeling you have for someone in the moment. Love is strong feeling that can be hurtful from time to time. Because when it comes to lust, there are no feelings afterwards. But when there is love, there are a lot feeling. Love will make a very pleasurable to one another. This is the difference between love and lust. Love endures all things as stated in Corinthians 13:7. Love will cover a multitude of sins. But in a relationship it has to be a compromise in love no matter what.

CHAPTER 9
Triumphs of My Friends with Difficult Medical Conditions

What Is Kidney Disease? UNDERSTANDING
KIDNEY DISEASE

It damages your kidneys to the point where it can lead to
complications with blood pressure and blood filtration.

When your kidneys are damaged, they cannot filter the waste products and fluids in your body. This results in swelling in ankles, vomiting, weakness, poor sleep habits and shortness of breath. Without treatment, this can lead to life threatening consequences such as acute kidney problems and kidney failure.

What is Acute Kidney Problems?

Acute Kidney problem is when your kidneys suddenly stops functioning. The cause could be due to the lack of blood flow, direct damage to the organs or when urine is backed up.

This can lead to complications such as septic shock, enlarged prostate, and the breakdown of muscle tissues due to the lack of protein.

My best friend Tiffany Joyce Robinson has been my friend since 1999 in high school but reconnected in 2007 when she started working for the Transportation Co. that I ride with. From this experience, we've had a lot of conversations and then is when I realized she was diagnosed with a kidney condition that made her very weak at times and made it hard for her to function. I spent a lot of time praying that she would get a kidney transplant. They thought I had a stomach virus at age 7 but my mom new it was deeper. Two years later, all our prayers had gotten answered.

She's a very nice person and anyone who gets to know her would absolutely love her and our friendship has expanded because both of us have had obstacles to overcome in life. She was misdiagnosed because they kept telling her she had a cold. She knew it was much more. Every time her mother looked at her it was as if she was far worse off.

Two Hearts

Robert E. Cohen
April 18, 2010
Tiffany Joyce

Two hearts connected together as one by an unexplainable bond that can never broken any natural force on earth. This bond is extremely special between people who are open. Honest, and understanding of each other feelings and respects each other point of view whether or not they agree they can and always will engage in intelligent. You inspire thought-provoking dialogue with my closes friend next to God and my earthly father. My best friend loves you. You will always hold an extremely special place in my heart as well as my life.

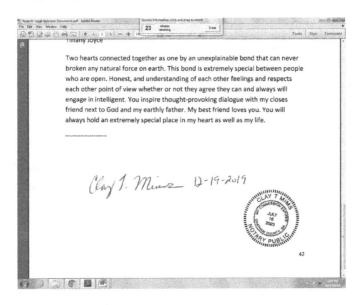

Robert Cohen

My friend Nene suffers from mild cerebral palsy which affects her walking. When I found out we had the same diagnosis with a different type, it really elated me because it let me know I'm not the only one that has cerebral palsy even though mine is a more severe type than hers. I have a lot of love and respect for her because we go through a lot of the same battles and have to overcome the same triumphs.

What is Cerebral Palsy?

Cerebral Palsy is a neurological condition involving muscle and body coordination. This is when brain damage occurs in an infant that happens during pregnancy, during delivery or not long after delivery.

There are several types of cerebral palsy and

Cerebral palsy is a neurological condition that affects muscle coordination and body movement. Cerebral palsy is an umbrella term for several symptoms because, unlike Down syndrome, it does not have a singular cause. Cerebral palsy is caused by brain damage occurring either during pregnancy, during delivery, or shortly after delivery. There are several different types of cerebral palsy, each classified by the way in which they affect the individual.

Because there are so many different factors as to the cause of cerebral palsy, each case is as individual as the person affected. The symptoms and severity of cerebral palsy can range from mild, barely noticeable effects,

Robert Cohen

to severe, in which the individual has extremely poor motor skills.

My special friend, with whom I've had a relationship since 2007, is one that I first met because we were trying to find ways to help her raise money to help her receive a kidney transplant. We always have had a great communicating relationship. We can come to each other about anything at any time. She is one of the most kind-hearted sweet people I know.

Roberts 34th Birthday Celebration (My friend Devon took her time after coming back from a trip and made me a beautiful birthday cake) ☺☺

Special Friendship

The Special friendship

is one that is kind,

loving, and heartfelt.

A friendship

in each person involved can feel each other's

love and respect for the friendship equally

between the persons in the friendship.

This friendship does not involve a lot of tangibles

or buying things for each other,

but rather being there for each other,

praying for each other,

and bearing each other's burdens

like it declares in God's word and the unconditional agape love

that should be spread from people to people,

city to city, state to state, country to country and nation to nation.

I'm blessed to have a friend that fits this description. I love you.

Dedication ~ Devon Jacobs.

What is end-stage kidney disease?

Key points

End-stage kidney or renal disease (ESRD) is the final stage of chronic kidney disease in which the kidneys no longer function well enough to meet the needs of daily life.

People with diabetes or hypertension have the highest risk of developing ESRD.

Robert, Brittany and Ariana at Finish Line the day before Robert's 34th Birthday just taking a swag photo.

Robert's 34ᵗʰ Birthday Party! We had a blast!

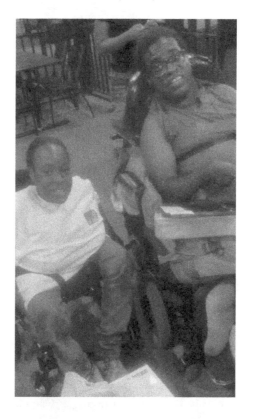

Robert Cohen

CHAPTER 10
Inspirational Speeches

G.E.D/Graduation Speech

As you embark on the next chapter of your life look back upon this accomplishment and reflect upon what it took for you to get to this point. Remember those who helped you along the way on this journey and remember to thank them for everything they did to help you reach this point.

As graduates look at this point in your life as an ending but also as a beginning now that you have received the book of knowledge you have obtained and apply it to your life to aid you in seeking gainful employment. Realize as you have worked to reach your goals each of you will have obstacles that you had to endure and overcome. Perseverance is each of your ability to move from one level of your life to another. Much like all of you, I also had obstacles to persevere in life. Being born with a development disability called cerebral palsy sometimes made it hard for me to see myself moving to the next level in my life because I was worried about how people would perceive me. I didn't want people to see the wheelchair and have preconceived notions about my learning ability simply because I had a physical disability. But with hard work, dedication, and the help given to me by God, my family, and my friends enabled me to proceed through the obstacles that I felt held me back the most. Like me, you all must also apply hard work and dedication in your life to be successful and reach the next level. For some, that would mean continuing school to get a higher degree and for others that means being dedicated to a job search until finding what it is you want to do in life. In conclusion, whichever path you choose, do your best and preserver.

Aspire to Persevere

Perseverance is each of your ability to move from one level of your life to another. Much like all of you, I also had obstacles to persevere in life. Being born with a development disability called cerebral palsy sometimes made it hard for me to see myself persevering to the next level in my life because I was worried about how people would perceive me. I didn't want people to see the wheelchair and have preconceived notions about my learning ability simply because I had a physical disability. But with hard work, dedication, and the help given to me by God, my family, and my friends enabled me to preserver through the obstacles that I felt held me back the most. Like me, you all must also apply hard work and dedication in your life to preserver and reach the next level. For some, that would mean continuing school to get a higher degree and for others that means being dedicated to a job search until finding what it is you want to do in life. Whichever path you choose, do your best and persevere to the next level of your life.

Trials and Tribulations

(Acknowledge pulpit)

Coming from the book of Job, sharing how education is the key and should be your focus. If you don't work hard for what you want, you may lose everything you have. (Book of **Job**) **verses 9-12** in **Chapter 1**.

⁹ "Does Job fear God for nothing?" Satan replied. ¹⁰ "Have you not put a hedge around him and his household and everything he has? You have blessed the work of his hands, so that his flocks and herds are spread throughout the land. ¹¹ But now stretch out your hand and strike everything he has, and he will surely curse you to your face."

¹² The LORD said to Satan, "Very well, then, everything he has is in your power, but on the man himself do not lay a finger." Then Satan went out from the presence of the LORD. NIV

Even though trials may come, that which doesn't kill you only makes you stronger. Sometimes we have to go through tests and trials to get what God has in store for us.

Without gaining the knowledge that you need it'll be hard to gain wealth. Not knowing what direction you're going is a trying place to be in. Trying to obtain things before it's time for you to have them is like being the prodigal son who demanded his share of his inheritance while his father was still living and then wastes it all with careless living. This is in **Luke 15:13-14**. ¹³ "Not long after that, the younger son got together all he had, set off for a distant country and there squandered his wealth in wild living. [14] After he had spent everything, there was a severe famine in that whole country, and he began to be in need. NIV

Sometimes you have to be patient and wait on your blessing b/c some Christians don't like to wait, but remember patience is a virtue and the trying of your faith works patience. That comes from **James 1:3**. [3] because you know that the testing of your faith produces perseverance. NIV

Having patience is not always an easy thing to do but sometimes when you have patience your blessing ends up being greater than what it originally was because you were patient and waited on the Lord to answer you; therefore, the Lord was willing to bless you abundantly and above with more than what you thought. **Ephesians Chapter 3:20** [20] "Now to him who is able to do immeasurably more than all we ask or imagine, according to his power that is at work within us..." NIV

Isaiah 40:31 "They that wait on the Lord shall renew their strength." NIV

If you rush trying to get something that God told you to wait on, it can cause you to have to stay in the storm longer than you were supposed to be there, because you did not do it the way God meant for it to be done and explained to you how to do it. So sometimes you get what you ask for.

Like the Parable of the Talents in **Matthew 25:13-20** (NIV) If you don't do the work to increase what you already have and take the time to study to get the knowledge then you're like the man with the one talent who took it and buried it in the ground and wasted it. Basically, you're wasting your time and your talent. Talent would be money in this case as well. Ultimately you're not doing anything to better yourself therefore it's difficult for you to have anything because you're not willing to work for it. The other two slaves took their talents and multiplied it. This is more so what you would want to do in life. These two took what they knew and what they had and were able to work and multiply what they had. When you work for what you want, you're able to multiply what you have and have it in greater abundance because you are willing to do the work.

Taking what you have and burying it is not losing but not gaining either. You have to take what you have and gain something with it. Proverbs says in all thy getting get understanding. **Proverbs 4:7** Wisdom is the principal thing; therefore, get wisdom: and with all thy getting, get understanding. KJV

In Closing, as youth in today's society education is the best thing for you to get because without gaining the knowledge it's harder for you to progress and move forward in life. Take my life as an example because I was able to do much with all of my physical limitations but I never gave up and I never let my disability have me. I have the disability and I am able to work through it. I do not let the physical bother me; I let each day worry about itself and trust God and let God have His way in my life.

CHAPTER 11
Inspirational Quotes

"Each day we wake up, God's power shines in your life and our light should shine to bless others always."
— Robert E. Cohen

"Your circumstances shouldn't define your life. The potential of the person should determine their success."
— Robert E. Cohen

"Be a blessing to those you can bless."
-Robert E. Cohen

"Your faith determines your patience, your patience determines your attitude, and your attitude determines your aptitude."
-Robert E. Cohen

"If you love yourself enough to believe in your dreams, you can achieve."
-Robert E. Cohen

CHAPTER 12
Achievements

Certificate of License

THIS IS TO CERTIFY

ROBERT COHEN

Who has given evidence that God has called him into
THE GOSPEL MINISTRY
we Licensed to preach the Gospel as he may have opportunity,
and to exercise his gifts in the work of the Ministry

by **First African Baptist Church**
at **Savannah, Georgia**
on the Twenty-sixth *day of* March *in the year of Our Lord* Two-Thousand Five

Rev. Thurmond N. Tillman, Pastor

March 26, 2006

March 28, 2015

CHAPTER 13
Press Releases

Double Book Signing To Be Held

Robert Cohen

On March 14, 2014 at 6:00pm at the Sentient Bean located at 13 E. Park Ave. local author Robert Cohen will host a double book signing. Cohen will have books on hand: Joys, Fears, and Tears for $10 and Faceoff: *Men vs. Women Needs, Wants, & Desires* for $15.

The public is invited to this event.
From: Robert Cohen
    (912) 844-1822
    Recohen1821@yahoo.com
For: Robert E. Cohen, Savannah Author

I Have Marks to Make Event: The Triple Book Signing

On December 7, 2014, Robert E. Cohen will host a book signing for his newest publication, Physically Challenged, But Mentally Determined. Cohen is not just your regular author; overcoming obstacles of a different type have made him all the more resilient. Among other features will be his two previous publications Joys, Fears & Tears which was his first book of poems which shared emotions of love, hurt and triumphs, as well as Men vs. Women: Needs, Wants & Desires inspired by the honest input of men and women just like you and I. This book signing will take place at The Jepson Center Telfair Museum, 207 West York Street, 2 o'clock in the afternoon.

From: Robert Cohen
    (912) 844-1822
    Recohen1821@yahoo.com
For: Robert E. Cohen, Savannah Author

I Have Marks to Make Art Exhibit: Book Signing

On December 12, 2015, Robert E. Cohen will host a book signing for his newest publication, *Soul of Love*. Adding another to his collection, Cohen is not just your regular author; overcoming obstacles of a different type have made him all the more resilient. Among other features will be his three previous publications *Joys, Fears & Tears*, which was his first book of his life story as well as *Men vs. Women: Needs, Wants & Desires* inspired by the honest input of men and women just like you and I. *Inspiration: Physically Challenged but Mentally Determined* is a book to inspire youth that with the help of God, hard work and dedication, anything is possible. The newly featured book, *Soul of Love* is a collection of poems sharing emotions of love, hurt and triumphs. This book signing will take place at The Jepson Center Telfair Museum, 207 West York Street, 2 o'clock in the afternoon.

From: Robert Cohen
    (912) 844-1822
    Recohen1821@yahoo.com
For: Robert E. Cohen, Savannah Author

Wheels Poet Open Mic & Book Signing

On April 8, 2017, Robert E. Cohen will host a book signing for all of his publications. Cohen is not just your regular author; overcoming obstacles of a different type have made him all the more resilient. Among those featured will be his four publications *Joys, Fears & Tears,* which was his first book of his life story as well as *Men vs. Women: Needs, Wants & Desires* inspired by the honest input of men and women just like you and I. *Inspiration: Physically Challenged but Mentally Determined* is a book to inspire youth that with the help of God, hard work and dedication, anything is possible. His latest *Soul of Love,* is a collection of poems sharing emotions of love, hurt and triumphs. This book signing will take place at Indulge Coffee, 1305 Barnard St., Savannah, GA 31401, 12:30 in the afternoon until 3 o'clock.

the savannahtribune

norwalkgirl likes this

1h

- the savannahtribune Wheels Poet Open Mic Booksigning

Wheels Poet Open Mic and Booksigning featuring Robert Cohen will be held on Saturday, April 8, 2017 12:30-3:00 pm at Indulge Coffee Shop, located at 1305 Barnard St. For more information call (912) 509-0564.

Robert Cohen was born on July 9, 1982 and although he was diagnosed with cerebral palsy only a year later, he never let that stop him from achieving his goals. Cohen is a native of Savannah, Georgia. He was educated in Chatham County Public Schools and received his high school diploma in 2001. He continued his education at Savannah State University from 2001 through 2005 when he earned his of Bachelor's in Science in Sociology and minored in Psychology.

CHAPTER 14
Book Articles

Local Author Has Overcome Obstacles and Wants to Encourage Others

2011-01-19 / Social & Community News

Robert Cohen

"This book describes a lot of things that I've been through in my life. It allows other people to be encouraged by the struggles that I've been able to overcome. Being born with Cerebral Palsy has been a very triumphant experience for me. I believe that this book will help others to see what I have to deal with on a daily basis."

Robert Cohen is a Motivational Speaker and writer of a book of poetry inspired by life experiences. Cohen is a native of Savannah Georgia and grew up in the Chatham County School system.

He received a undergraduate Bachelor of Science in Sociology with a minor in Psychology from Savannah State University in December 2005. On March 2006 Cohen received his license to minister.

For the past ten years Cohen has worked for the City of Savannah as a Summer Camp Counselor and is on the Board of Directors for the Chatham Savannah Citizens Advocacy.

In his role for the Chatham Savannah Citizens Advocacy, he has developed and implemented programs to assist the disabled better their life skills.

He is excited to be a member of GoodWill Good Guides mentoring program. He is also a part of a Cerebral Palsy support group.

As a writer Robert is constantly seeking creative ways to foster a dynamic learning environment and to promote life to those less fortunate through his books.

Spotted®: Jepson Center exhibit showcases artwork from Savannah rehabilitation programs

Posted: December 8, 2013 - 9:41pm | **Updated:** December 9, 2013 - 7:44am

Back | Next

Robert Cohen, right, reads from his work Sunday at the Jepson Center for the Arts' annual "I Have Marks to Make" exhibit and program. Assisting Cohen, a Savannah writer born with cerebral palsy, is Telfair Museums employee Glenna Barlow. (Dash Coleman/Savannah Morning News)

When Heather Rhea Green's career with the Navy was cut short in 2006 when she was diagnosed with fibromyalgia, it marked the end of one of her lifelong dreams.

"When I got separated (from the Navy), it kind of tore me up," the 28-year-old new mother said Sunday standing next to her oil and acrylic painting "Amazon's Victory" at the Jepson Center for the Arts. "And this painting has gone through a few iterations on the same canvas."

The painting, which she said started a lot darker, depicts a woman's figure in a powerful pose with outstretched arms surrounded by bursting light.

Though Green and her husband have only been in town about a year, she's wanted to move to Savannah since she was 17.

"My other big dream besides the Navy was to have one of my paintings displayed at the Jepson Center," she said. "And it's been 11 years, and it's finally happened. I feel like I finally proved all those people who believed in me right."

Green's painting is one of many being featured in the 19th annual "I Have Marks to Make" exhibition, which features the works of artists from local rehabilitation programs. Works from all ages are displayed.

On Sunday, the exhibition, which is on display until Jan. 5, opened with a reception and performance session featuring readings of poetry and other writing and music.

"It's just an event that we really anticipate and one I think that really speaks to the importance of art in our lives," Harry DeLorme, senior curator of education at the Telfair Museums, told the crowd gathered.

Robert Cohen, 31, was born with cerebral palsy and is confined to a wheelchair, but the Savannahian has worked to earn a degree in sociology and write three books. His poetry readings brought the performance section of Sunday's event toward a close.

"Though being born with cerebral palsy, I've never let that stop me," Cohen said afterward. "My thing is all about making a difference and inspiring other people to ... believe in their dreams and stay the course. Whatever it is they're trying to do, it can be achieved, because I'm a living witness of it."

Hubie Cowart, 69, suffered a stroke two years ago, and making art has been therapeutic. Cowart's mixed-media piece "Road Trip" features images of motorcycles, pieces of his life and brings travel to the mind.

The piece took Cowart about three months to complete, and he was happy to have it displayed at the Jepson.

"It's good," Cowart said of having his work featured in the exhibit. "It's right."

Savannah man who overcame odds to become poet and author will headline Spitfire Saturday

21 Nov 2016

Poet and author <u>Robert Cohen</u> is determined to overcome the odds he faces in life. Born July 9, 1982, Cohen was diagnosed with cerebral palsy when he was just 1 year old. Although he uses a wheelchair, he has never let his disability stop him from achieving his goals.

On Nov. 25, Cohen will headline the <u>Spitfire Saturday Open Mic and Showcase</u>, hosted by the Spitfire Poetry Group. The event is held the last Saturday of every month, featuring a mixture of music, poetry, visual art and other artistic forms of expression.

"I'll be the featured artist that night," Cohen says. "I'll also do a book signing and selling that night, as well."

A Savannah native, Cohen was educated in Chatham County public schools, graduating from high school in 2001. He went on to earn a Bachelor of Science degree at <u>Savannah State University</u> in 2005, majoring in sociology and minoring in psychology.

Raised within the community of the historic First African Baptist Church in downtown Savannah, Cohen became a licensed minister at the age of 23. He is a member of First Jerusalem Baptist Church on the west side of Savannah near Liberty City, where he serves on the greeter's ministry and assists in group ministering.

For the past 12 years, Cohen has worked for the city as a summer camp youth counselor. He counsels children ages 6-13 on many topics, ranging from drug and alcohol prevention to the importance of staying in school. In 2007, Cohen became a volunteer with Chatham-Savannah Citizen Advocacy. He serves as the chairman of the board of directors.

In addition, Cohen has been a volunteer with the therapeutic program at the John S. Delaware Recreation Center and worked for Goodwill as a mentor and at Memorial University Medical Center as an outpatient escort. Six years ago, Cohen published his first book, "Joys, Fears and Tears," poetry about his life experiences, including living with cerebral palsy, family situations and relationships with friends and female acquaintances.

His second book is "Faceoff: Men vs. Women's Needs, Wants and Desires." His third book is "Inspiration: Physically Challenged but Mentally Determined."

His latest book is "The Soul of Love." "This book describes how couples determine how to handle situations in a relationship," Cohen says. "You'll find different points of views in regards to loving one another, how to start and develop a family within a relationship and much more."

At the event, the books will sell for $10-$15.

At 3 p.m. Dec. 10, Cohen will sign books during "I Have Marks to Make" at the Jepson Center, 207 W. York St. For Cohen, the secret of his success is no secret at all.

"Belief in God, strong faith, a willingness to never give in," he says. "Your circumstances shouldn't define your life. The potential of the person should determine their success."

Posted December 15, 2016 09:06 pm - Updated December 16, 2016 09:32 am
By Ben Goggins

Looking for Pearls: 'I Have Marks to Make' explores possibilities of therapeutic art

On the stage in his wheelchair, Robert Cohen captured the spirit of "Marks to Make." He has appeared in previous years and read from the books he has written. But he said, "This year I am going to read from my heart."

He is 34 years old and has cerebral palsy. When he was born, his mother was told that he would probably not live a week. But he did and has been writing since age 11. What he said to the artists in the audience was a powerful motivation.

"Who better to tell your story than you? Vets, you are still here for a reason."

Mahatma Gandhi said simply, "What we can do, we will try to do." Cohen's closing words were along those lines.

"Be a blessing to those you can bless."

Ben Goggins, a retired marine biologist, lives on Tybee Island. He can be reached at bengoggins9@gmail.com

Posted: Tuesday, November 3, 2015 11:27 am
The Story of Robert Cohen
By: Jhasmine Wade

The story of Robert Cohen

Robert Cohen was born on July 9, 1982 and although he was diagnosed with cerebral palsy only a year later, he never let that stop him from achieving his goals. Cohen is a native of Savannah, Georgia. He was educated in Chatham County Public Schools and received his high school diploma in 2001. He continued his education at Savannah State University from 2001 through 2005 when he earned his of Bachelor's in Science in Sociology and minored in Psychology. Robert Cohen was brought up in the historic First African Baptist Church in Downtown Savannah.

At the age of 23, Cohen received his license in Ministry. He is now a member of First Jerusalem Baptist Church on the Westside of Savannah near Liberty City where he serves on the Greeter's Ministry and he also assists in Group Ministering. In 2007, he started volunteering with the Chatham Savannah Citizen's Advocacy and joined the Board of Directors. He has been an active member for the past three years and served as Chairman of the Board of Directors. Robert Cohen has worked for the City of Savannah for the past 12 years as a summer camp youth counselor where he counseled children aged 6-13 on many topics from drug and alcohol prevention to the importance of staying in school. Cohen has done lots of volunteer work, such as working with the Therapeutic Program at the John S. Delaware recreation center in 2006, working for Goodwill as a mentor in 2010 and working at Memorial Health University as an out-patient escort in 2011.

In November of 2010, Cohen published his first book, "Joys, Fears and Tears" which is a compilation of his life experiences in the form of poetry. He expresses how he feels about situations that occurred in his lifetime; from living with cerebral palsy, to different family situations, to relationships with friends and female acquaintances. In November of 2013, Cohen published, "Inspiration: Physically Challenged but Mentally Determined," a book written to inspire others that with the help of God, hard work and dedication, anything is possible. In December of 2013, Cohen published, "Faceoff: Men vs. Women Needs, Wants, & Desires." This book discusses relationships and situations that couples go through in these relationships. In March of 2015, Cohen became ordained as a licensed Minister.

December 12, 2015, Robert E. Cohen will host a book signing for his newest publication, Soul of Love. Adding another to his collection, Cohen is not just your regular author; overcoming obstacles of a different type have made him all the more resilient. Among other features will be his three previous publications Joys, Fears & Tears, which was his first book of his life story as well as Men vs. Women: Needs, Wants & Desires inspired by the honest input of men and women just like you and I. Inspiration: Physically Challenged but Mentally Determined is a book to inspire youth that with the help of God, hard work and dedication, anything is possible.

The newly featured book, Soul of Love is a collection of poems sharing emotions of love, hurt and triumphs. This book signing will take place at The Jepson Center Telfair Museum, 207 West York Street, 2 o'clock in the afternoon.

Wheels Poet Open Mic Booksigning

By Savannah Tribune | on April 05, 2017

Robert Cohen was born on July 9, 1982 and although he was diagnosed with cerebral palsy only a year later, he never let that stop him from achieving his goals. Cohen is a native of Savannah, Georgia. He was educated in Chatham County Public Schools and received his high school diploma in 2001. He continued his education at Savannah State University from 2001 through 2005 when he earned his of Bachelor's in Science in Sociology and minored in Psychology. Robert Cohen was brought up in the historic First African Baptist Church in Downtown Savannah.. In November of 2010, Cohen published his first book, "Joys, Fears and Tears" which is a compilation of his life experiences in the form of poetry. He expresses how he feels about situations that occurred in his lifetime; from living with cerebral palsy, to different family situations, to relationships with friends and female acquaintances. In November of 2013, Cohen published, "Inspiration: Physically Challenged but Mentally Determined," a book written to inspire others that with the help of God, hard work and dedication, anything is possible. In December of 2013, Cohen published, "Faceoff: Men vs. Women Needs, Wants, & Desires." This book discusses relationships and situations that couples go through in these relationships. In March of 2015, Cohen became ordained as a licensed Minister.

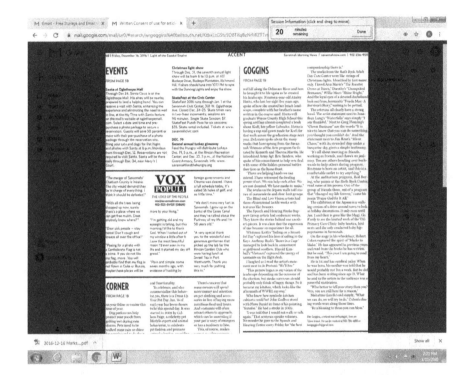

I Have Marks to Make
Jepson at Christmas

Last Saturday was opening day at the Jepson for the 22nd annual "I Have Marks to Make" exhibition. The halls were decked with bright works of art hung like Christmas ornaments by members of a great big family.

Like every treasured family ornament, every piece of art holds a story, and these were hung like Christmas cards from friends and loved ones. Walking through the halls, with art on either side, was secure and familiar, old and new, déjà vu.

It was a free Jepson Family Day, and the kids seemed especially excited. The annual exhibition is like a Christmas gift from the Telfair, a tradition where the presents are art from a hundred secret Santas. Every piece is a present to be studied, the wrapping and what's inside waiting to be discovered.

The Exhibition bills itself as "showcasing the therapeutic power of artmaking," and it features artwork from individuals of all ages with disabilities or in rehabilitation from illness or injury. More than half the works in the exhibition were created in Telfair's outreach sessions to health and wellness organizations throughout the community. And the rest is art from good kids in good art programs in good schools.

Mid-afternoon there was a program in the Neises Auditorium where a number of the artists took the stage. In his welcoming remarks Telfair curator Harry DeLorme captured the true meaning of Christmas, the true meaning of what the various programs mean to the people of Savannah.

He stressed how art helps us all physically and mentally. He had all the artists and writers present raise their hands. He had one, Tommy Purvis, stand and take a bow. Purvis was one of the first participants in "I Have Marks to Make."

In 1993 Purvis, a welder all his life, suffered a debilitating head injury. After his accident he enrolled in what is now known as Goodwill's ADVANCE Acquired Brain Injury program. Throughout the years of his rehabilitation, he began to create art. He recovered fully and returned to work.

"Making art by welding became a real motivation for me." A group of fourth-graders from Gadsden Elementary were fascinated by two of his large sculptures. One was an elegant egret stepping through cattails and spider webs. Innocent enough. But the other was a cobra arching above a basket, tongue flicking and eyes unblinking.

I didn't want to get too close to it or make any sudden moves. Not to sound too much like Brian Fellow, but that cobra looked like a candidate for a "Night at the Museum" Telfair sequel. The Gadsden kids sat down and eagerly listened as Purvis told them how he finds metal and transforms it into hummingbirds, dandelions, spiders, and snakes.

But back to the auditorium program. DeLorme introduced three artists from the Savannah Center for Blind and Low Vision. Jessica Thomas described how she has been a woman of low vision for eight years. She described how Telfair instructors Autumn Gary and Trelani Duncan had helped her "paint a new landscape, for myself, and for others to see."

Dale Walker described a forgotten scene from his sighted days of a red hill along the Delaware River and how he brought it to life again as he created his landscape. Nineteen-year-old Anzley Hutto, who lost her sight five years ago, spoke of how she created her beach landscape, complete with her brother's name written in the coarse sand.

Hutto will graduate Wayne County High School this spring and has almost completed a book about Kodi, her yellow Labrador. It moves through Kodi's puppy days, her training as a service dog, her life with Hutto, and her record of perfect attendance. Hutto is having a cap and gown made for Kodi for that walk across the graduation stage next year.

DeLorme spoke about the many works that have sprung from the Savannah Veterans of the Arts program facilitated by Kenneth and Theresa Martin. He introduced US Army Sergeant Eric Sanders who spoke of his commitment to help vets deal with some of the hidden personal battles they face on the home front.

"There are helping hands we can extend. I have witnessed the healing power of art. We can help each other. We are not daunted. We have marks to make."

The works on the Jepson walls told stories of camaraderie and close-knit groups. The Blind and Low Vision artists had three-dimensional tactile works with textures like frescoes.

The Speech and Hearing Stroke Support Group artists had exuberant works. They knew the stories behind each other's pieces. It was clear that the expression of one became an experience for all.

Whitman Keith's "Sailing on a Beautiful Day" captured his love of sailing in the Keys. Anthony Bush's "Bears in a Cage" managed to look back in amusement at girlfriend conflicts. Harold Kimball's "Vietnam" captured the energy of moments on the flight deck.

I laughed as I read the artist's statement next to Jo Poston's "We'll See." "This picture began as my vision of the landscape depending on the outcome of the election, but stroke survivors should probably only think of happy things. So it became my kitchen, which looks like the aftermath of WWIII anyway." Who knew how symbolic kitchen cabinets could be?

John Godbee stood with Flora Daniel in front of his painting "Sunrise." He had a stroke in 2009. "I was told that I would not walk or talk again." That sentence speaks volumes. No wonder he goes to the Speech and Hearing Center every Friday for "the best companionship there is."

The works from the Ruth Byck Adult Day Care Center were like strings of Christmas lights. Identified by first name only, I loved Ann Marie's "The Rooster Crows at Dawn," Dorothy's "Unrequited Romance," Willie Mae's "Shine Bright." And the loyal eyes of a devoted dachshund look out from Jeremiah's "Frieda Mae: A Survivor's Story," waiting to be petted.

The veterans all clearly have a strong bond. The artist statement next to Jonathan Lang's "Waterfalls" says simply "I am thankful." Next to Greg Fleming's "Clown Business" are the words "It is nice to know that you can do something you thought you couldn't do." And the statement next to Jim Rose's "Silent Chaos," with its stranded ship under a turquoise sky, gives a simple testimony. "It's all about meeting as friends, working as friends, and there's no jealousy. You see others bending over backwards to help others during progress. Everyone is born an artist, and this is a comfortable outlet to try anything."

At the auditorium program Rod Boring, who paints at the Ruth Byck Center, read some of his poems. Out of the group of friends there, out of a program that "changed my life forever," came his poem "Praise God for It All."

The exhibition at the Jepson is a walking version of a drive around town to look at holiday decorations. It only runs until January 1 and then is gone like the Magi. Go if only to see the knitted work of the VA's Primary Care Clinic: baby booties, bird nests, and the only crocheted baby hippopotamus in Savannah.

On the stage in his wheelchair Robert Cohen captured the spirit of "Marks to Make." He has appeared in previous years and read from the books he has written. But he said that "this year I am going to read from my heart."

He is 34 years old and has cerebral palsy. When he was born, his mother was told that he would probably not live a week. But he did and has been writing since age 11. What he said to the artists in the audience was a powerful motivation.

"Who better to tell your story than you? Vets, you are still here for a reason." Mahatma Gandhi said simply, "What we can do, we will try to do." Cohen's closing words were along those lines. "Be a blessing to those you can bless."

CHAPTER 15
Speaking Opportunities

Love, Believe, Achieve Brochure

Purpose

"My purpose in life is to motivate and encourage others in many different ways whether it is through my faith in God, or education and knowledge. I believe in encouraging individuals in my community to believe and achieve their dreams."
Robert E. Cohen

My Biography

Robert Cohen was born on July 9, 1982 and although he was diagnosed with cerebral palsy only a year later, he never let that stop him from achieving his goals. In 2001, he earned his high school diploma, and in 2005 his Bachelor's degree in Sociology. Robert is an avid philanthropist in his community. He is always volunteering with different organizations such as the City of Savannah, John S. Delaware Recreation Center, and at the Chatham Savannah Citizen's Advocacy.

Publications

Joys Fears & Tears
(Journal of life events)

MEN VS. WOMEN
Needs, Wants, and Desires

Inspiration: Physically Challenged but Mentally Determined

Soul of Love

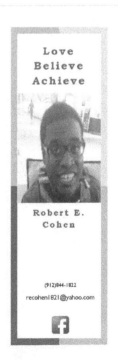

Love
Believe
Achieve

Robert E.
Cohen

(912)844-1822

recohen1821@yahoo.com

Session One: Turning an Obstacle into a Stepping Stone

- My disability made me focus more on becoming a God communicator. I needed to make myself understand.

- This led to writing poetry and being published.

- When I was alone I wrote my thoughts and feelings down with a computer. Writing allows me to express more clearly than speaking.

- Accept limitations, but build on your strengths.

- Obstacles have led me to communicate, and help others. My disability made this possible, to have more empathy, to encourage others. We all have obstacles we have to persevere through.

Session Two: Having a Strong Support System

- Parents have always been a strong influence in my life. It led me to being a strong and successful person myself.

- If not your parents or family, who in your life, can encourage you? It makes a world of difference to have someone.

- It unlocks your potential for the future.

- Find a mentor: Big Brothers or Big Sisters, My Brother's Keeper, Boy Scouts, Girl Scouts, and teachers.

Session Three: Education- Knowledge is the Key to Success.

- Education is on the decline among certain parts of our population.

- Bachelors degree is now equal to a High School Diploma.

- The way to gain access to resources is to do well in school.

- My disability created a barrier to education, not being able to write made it difficult to make my thoughts coherent and organized. Especially in math, different formulas were difficult because I could not write. I knew without education there would not be much that I could do.

- Being able to go to class and hear education made a substantial difference.

- Book smart doesn't equal drive to move forward.

Session Four: Achieving Goals that seem Unachievable

- Black males often don't take full advantage of the opportunities presented to them in society, making it difficult for them to succeed. If you can get through high school and get a post secondary education there's no telling what you can do.

- I've written three books and I am a chairman of an organization that does important work in our community.

- Take the time to plant a seed, water the seed, and feed it. You can reach unthinkable achievements and success in your life, personality and professionally.

Chapter 16
Published Books

(published December 1, 2013)

Here's a collection of poems about my life story which can include my joy, my fears and my tears because that's what human life is all about.

Inspiration: Physically Challenged
but Mentally Determined

Robert Cohen

(published September 20, 2013)

This book will give youth and young adults hope and vision to believe in their dreams and not give up on life.

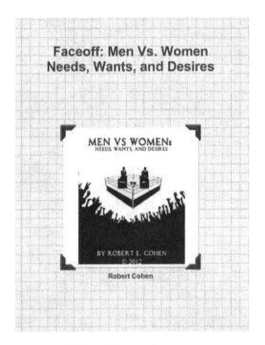

(published November 1, 2013)

In this book you will understand how to evaluate and see relationship from each other point of view, as well as understand other types of relationships.

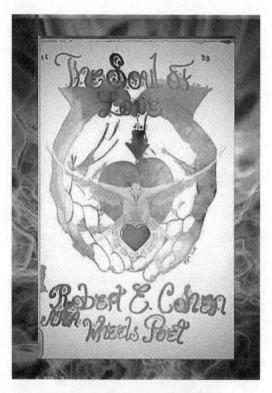

(published October 1, 2015)

The Soul of Love is a compilation of poems that relate readers to love and relationship. You will explore the description, as I see it, of a person exploring and experiencing the diversification of love in relationships.

Chapter 17
Other Friends

My Friend Jamie

The Day We Met in the Student Union I was actually scared to go up and talk to her because I thought she wasn't going to be very becoming of me. She was pretty receptive and we actually had a nice conversation. I appreciated the conversation we had and I hope to get to know her in the coming semester and the coming years.

The Sweetest Friendship

January 23, 2016
Dedication: Terri House

The sweetest friendship is a deep heartfelt friendship that's very special to me. This friendship is very kind, caring, and loving. The person in my life is very intelligent, bold, and beautiful. She has the most open-minded and kindhearted personality of any friendship I've had, up to this point in my life. She always makes me smile at the beautiful sight of her. My heart skips a beat at the mere thought of her. We communicate very well in our friendship. The friendship brings joy to my heart and in my life. I feel a sense of calmness and peace and understanding in our friendship. I pray that God will continuously blessings on us and the friendship we have together. God bless you.

I love you,

Your Special Friend Robert Cohen

My Friend Treasure

We met about the end of February or early March of 2017. She was working at Wet Seal and she along with her employees were very receptive of me. So I tried to make sure I went to see her as much as time allowed. Wet Seal closed around April, then a month later she started managing Aeropostale in the mall. We reconnected and we really have a close bond. I really have a lot of love and respect for her. No matter what happens, we will always be friends.

Acknowledgements/ Influential People in my Life

I'd like to thank my mom Gladys Cohen because she's always instilled the driving force that keeps me moving.

My dad Robert L. Cohen because he always makes sure that I'm able to do what I feel like I needs to be done out in the community to become a better person.

Dicky Stone is a friend and mentor to me. He's the person I go to when I can't go to my parents.

My two sisters: my twin sister Robin Brown is the one who taught me how to defend myself. My sister Lakeisha Wilborn keeps me in line when I'm feeling down. Robin's husband my brother-in-law

Derwin Brown helps me to realize there are real people that care enough to help others he defines what a good man is for a woman because he treat my sister like a queen.

Brian Wilborn is a teacher and he's also an ordained minister, but also my brother-in-law. I look to him for spiritual guidance sometimes.

Shamonica McKinney-Small has been my friend since childhood and has always been there for me.

Joe Davis: He is the full service director at Savannah State University. We've been friends for about 5 years. In that time we have developed a really great friendship. He always looks out for me and makes sure I'm okay as far as life and my physical well-being. He looks out for my best interest. He wants me to do well. I acknowledge those who've impacted my life. I realize that if it had not been for these people, I would never act on dreams.

Tiffany Joyce-Robinson: She's one of my best friends. We went to high school together. She was born with a kidney disorder but like me she has never let that stop her. She's one of the most influential people in my life because she inspires me. We have a unique bond. I can tell her about my problems.

Keisha Richardson: I met Keisha in October of 2016 and we developed a nice relationship. We connect because our personality traits are similar.

Terri House: Terri is a great friend, someone I can talk to about things going on with me. We have a great relationship. We met in April 2015. We've been close ever since. I really value her friendship and the bond we share.

Evangelist Shawna Biggins: We previously went to the same church. Throughout the year and a half that I've known her we have become very close and able to talk about these things. We were ordained as ministers together.

Bishop Byron Curry: I met him in January of 2015, at a bible study that I was conducting that night. After I completed the study, he gave fall out commentary on what I was talking about. I visited his church in March 8, 2015 for the first time. We have a great relationship. He gives me spiritual advice and as well life advice. We feed off of each other.

He has helped me grow as a person. I hope our relationship grows to be better. He is one of my biggest supporters and whatever I do.

Paris Carter: We met Homecoming of 2016 at SSU. We had a very short conversation which involved me showing her my books and she really liked the two pages she read. The week before that Thanksgiving I saw her again and we reconnected. We've been close ever since. While on Christmas break, I called her and prayed with her and her sister and the prayer was more for her. I believe was more inspired by it because of the things I've been through and the things that I've been doing. They're both really great people and I blessed to have them both in my life.

Janae Jackson: We met around the middle of March-early April. She was sitting in the Student Union talking with some of her friends and I went to speak to all of them. She and I had a conversation. I showed her my books. She was really impressed by them. Three weeks later, I saw her working at the Chicken Shack on campus and we reconnected once again. She has been a great friend and a blessing to my life.

Charmele Thomas has been a great friend. We've had a friendship for about two years. We can communicate about almost anything. I really appreciate her friendship.

Tierra Kirk has been a great friend and always there when I need her. The conversations we have are really insightful and enjoyable. She has a beautiful smile that always makes me smiles as well. I appreciate her friendship in my life.

Jada Reeves is a great inspiration to my life. We have a great working and personal relationship. She's a blessing to my life and just an overall wonderful person to be around.

Sherica Steverson: I met her on July 12th of 2019. We started spending time together and no matter what happens we will always be friends and be there for one another.

Camille Jones: We met back in August of 2019 at the annual walk for homelessness event that took place at Lake Mayer in Savannah Ga. We had a mutual friend who was the host of the event. I have been getting my hair cut by her for the last 3 or 4 months. She is the best female barber that I have seen in a long time. No matter what she will always hold a very significant and special place in my heart.

Crystal Capers: She works at the document center at Savannah State University. She is always willing and ready to help me whenever I need it. I spent countless hours there printing books and flyers for my book events and she is always very loving and patient with me especially since my mother passed away two years ago.

Earl Mason: He works for Chatham Area Transit (CAT). He is a great driver and has over 30 years of experience with the company. We also formally attended the same church; First Jerusalem Missionary Baptist Church under the leadership of the late Gregory Alexander Tyson Sr.

Tiffany Thomas: We first met approximately 6 years ago when she was working at Macys Dept. store in the Oglethorpe Mall. We have had countless conversations about life's situations and have been able to help each one of our struggles. I have recently reconnected with her. She has always been very receptive and been willing to help me, we have even taken time out for us to pray and encourage one another.

In conclusion, I've been through a lot of trials and tribulations in my life; some good, some bad. Life never deals you a specific deck of cards. So you have to play the cards you're dealt understanding the fact that God knows what's best and he does everything for a reason. I've accomplished a lot over the past thirty-five years and I want the readers of my book to take my life and use it as testimony for their life and never give up on their dreams, hopes and aspirations. Even if you try and fail, God will always honor your effort. Try your best and no matter what the outcome is, you'll be successful no matter what.

About the Author

Robert Cohen was born on July 9, 1982 and although he was diagnosed with cerebral palsy only a year later, he never let that stop him from achieving his goals.

Cohen is a native of Savannah, Georgia. He was educated in Chatham County Public Schools and received his high school diploma in 2001. He continued his education at Savannah State University from 2001 through 2005 when he earned his of Bachelor's in Science in Sociology and minored in Psychology.

Robert Cohen was brought up in the historic First African Baptist Church in Downtown Savannah. At the age of 23, Cohen received his license in Ministry. He is now a member of First Jerusalem Baptist Church on the Westside of Savannah near Liberty City where he serves on the Greeter's Ministry and he also assists in Group Ministering.

In 2007, he started volunteering with the Chatham Savannah Citizen's Advocacy and joined the Board of Directors. He has been an active member for the past three years and served as Chairman of the Board of Directors.

Robert Cohen has worked for the City of Savannah for the past 12 years as a summer camp youth counselor where he counseled children aged 6-13 on many topics from drug and alcohol prevention to the importance of staying in school.

Cohen has done lots of volunteer work, such as working with the Therapeutic Program at the John S. Delaware recreation center in 2006, working Robert Cohen was born on July 9, 1982 and although he was diagnosed with cerebral palsy only a year later, he never let that stop him from achieving his goals.

Cohen is a native of Savannah, Georgia. He was educated in Chatham County Public Schools and received his high school diploma in 2001. He continued his education at Savannah State University from 2001 through 2005 when he earned his of Bachelor's in Science in Sociology and minored in Psychology.

Robert Cohen was brought up in the historic First African Baptist Church in Downtown Savannah. At the age of 23, Cohen received his license in Ministry. He is now a member of First Jerusalem Baptist Church on the Westside of Savannah near Liberty City where he serves on the Greeter's Ministry and he also assists in Group Ministering.

Cohen is currently a member of the Brandon Heart's International Church. Where he does motivational speaking, prayer, and devotional services.

In 2007, he started volunteering with the Chatham Savannah Citizen's Advocacy and joined the Board of Directors. He has been an active member for the past three years and served as Chairman of the Board of Directors.

Robert Cohen has worked for the City of Savannah for the past 12 years as a summer camp youth counselor where he counseled children aged 6-13 on many topics from drug and alcohol prevention to the importance of staying in school.

Cohen has done lots of volunteer work, such as working with the Therapeutic Program at the John S. Delaware recreation center in 2006, working for Goodwill as a mentor in 2010 and working at Memorial Health University as an out-patient escort in 2011.

In November of 2010, Cohen published his first book, "Joys, Fears and Tears" which is a compilation of his life experiences in the form of poetry. He expresses how he feels about situations that occurred in his lifetime; from living with cerebral palsy, to different family situations, to relationships with friends and female acquaintances.

In November of 2013, Cohen published, "Inspiration: Physically Challenged but Mentally Determined," a book written to inspire others that with the help of God, hard work and dedication, anything is possible.

In December of 2013, Cohen published, "Faceoff: Men vs. Women Needs, Wants, & Desires." This book discusses relationships and situations that couples go through in these relationships.

Finally, he has most recently written *Soul of Love* in December of 2015. It is a collection of love poems that discuss love in its different forms.

In March of 2015, Cohen became ordained as a licensed Minister.

Works Cited

American Bible Society. (2010). *Holy Bible: containing the Old and New Testaments: King James Version.* New York.

Khatri, Minesh. "Kidney Disease." *Kidney Disease,* 21 Dec. 2018, https://www.webmd.com/a-to-z-guides/understanding-kidney-disease-basic-information#1

What is Cerebral Palsy? (2016, September 16). Retrieved September 19, 2017, from https://symptomchecker.webmd.com/symptoms-a-z.

CPSIA information can be obtained
at www.ICGtesting.com
Printed in the USA
JSHW020353220722
28391JS00001B/7